RWANDA, A DIARY FROM HELL

To receive our
free catalogue,
please write to:

Piero Gribaudi Editore srl
Via C. Baroni, 190
20142 Milano
Italy
Phone +39-2-89302244 – Fax +39-2-89302376

Father Vito Misuraca

RWANDA

RWANDA
A DIARY FROM HELL

Introduction by
Piero Gheddo

Contributors:
Claudio Monici
Roberto Beretta
Rodolfo Casadei

Piero Gribaudi Editore
La Commerciale

Cover by Patrizia Sola

Cover photo by Nino Leto

ISBN 88-7152-361-X
First edition: December 1995
Original title: Ruanda, Diario dall'Inferno
© 1994 by Piero Gribaudi Editore S.r.l.
Via C. Baroni, 190 - 20142 Milan (Italy)
and Tipografia La Commerciale
Via Monte San Genesio, 7 - 20158 Milan (Italy)

Printed by:
INGRAF Industria Grafica S.r.l.
Via Monte San Genesio, 7 - 20158 Milan (Italy)
Tél. 2-6887193 - 6682051 - 6071180

WHY THIS BOOK?

Preface

This book is Father Vito Misuraca's diary, a Sicilian priest, who set his roots in Rwanda for over eighteen years, now. He wrote it during that terrible month, between April and May 1994. Father Vito, a parish priest in charge of some thirty orphans for four years in Kigali, capital city of Rwanda, has been taking down his notes day by day on his laptop computer, a tiny equipment, whose electronic whims one needs to master.

This is no ordinary diary. It is the real story of an immense tragedy which cost the lives of hundreds of thousands of people (the victims might be over one million), massacred with barbarous practices even for no specific reason. While peering out of the unsecure window of Nyanza orphanage (where he had taken shelter with his children after an adventurous and dangerous flight from the capital being bombed at the time), Father Vito simply wrote down a few brief notes. Maybe he only did it

7

to relieve his stress, maybe not to forget. Maybe even while having us in mind, so that we would also one day become aware of the tragedy.

At any rate, Father Vito did want to write this diary for his children. At the time he left, there were about 600 of them, while today they are 800, and more. The missionary will soon be back with them: he wants to rebuild - as soon as peace is restablished - the orphanage, building of which he had already started, but that some opponent gangs have now destroyed. That is because a "Father" never gives in.

While waiting to return, Father Vito, a front-line man used to the sort of loneliness that the solidarity of love often forces one into, actually hopes that the reader will understand and share the destiny of many innocent black brothers, at least in spirit. And if, moreover, anybody wishes to give his/her practical help to this missionary's work in Rwanda, he/she will find here all indications as to how to do it. No matter how substantial a check, will not save Africa, of course, none the less its children still deserve at least a drop of our opulence.

Roberto Beretta
Avvenire

Address:
DON VITO MISURACA
ORPHANAGE MËRE DU VERBE
P.O.B.. 2380 KIGALI - RWANDA
Bank:
DON VITO MISURACA
COMMERCIAL BANK OF RWANDA
N° 010 - 1064401 - 04
KIGALI - RWANDA

We thank the Italian newspaper AVVENIRE for correspondent Claudio Monici's reportage and Rodolfo Casadei's article, EPIPRESS/FAMIGLIA CRISTIANA, for Nino Leto's cover photo, and GRIBAUDI Publishing House for the editorial coordination and INGRAF company for the composition and printing.

9

WHAT CAN WE DO FOR RWANDA?

by Piero Gheddo

A prayer to be said every morning: "My Lord, please do not allow me to become accustomed to the horrors of the daily news, please give me the ability to respond emotionally, to react with indignation against the oppression exerted by the very man you created in your own image and likeness".

Both newspapers and television overwhelm us with their reports of massacres, rapes, genocides in heavy doses: Bosnia, Somalia, Sudan, Liberia, Cambodia, Afghanistan, Haiti, Angola, Mozambique and ... recently, Rwanda. We have run out of sensitivity, indignation, sympathy. News and pictures now pass by us like water running off a duck's back. We are experiencing for real what Mac Luhan, a communication theorist, had foreseen: the daily bombardment of messages soon acts like a massage on our consciences, which become indifferent. Three children being kidnapped and killed, that would touch us. A hundred thousand children

11

in the same situation do not touch us any more. Let's be honest: we are powerless over the horrors of these repeated genocides. We are still provoked to indignation as we remember the nazi pogrom of fifty years ago; but when considering the holocaust in Rwanda or the one carried out by Cambodian red Khmers (much worse in any sense), we merely write a couple newspaper articles and send a few planes to save a hundred children. And we simply abandon all the others (tens, hundreds of thousands) to their own fate.

What can we do? There actually is a third way we should follow all together and in all humility, and which lays between the skepticism of those who say that there is nothing we can do and the pharisaical attitude of those who, while being touched, quickly forget all about it. Our first duty consists in becoming instructed, and impassioned for human events as well as never loosing the ability of being indignant and of reacting effectively against whatever violence is being perpetrated against a human being.

This rather instant book, bringing together a missionary's diary and the correspondence of a journalist who travelled over to the spot to gain a direct experience, shows us the way to take.

Faith helps a lot. If I really believe that each single man, even the humblest one, holds within himself a sparkle of God's life, and, therefore, ontologically, has as many rights to live as I do, then I can't but feel some interest for him as well as love, and passion, while becoming available to help him, no matter how distant and unknown to me he might be. A white Father, who managed to escape from the Rwanda hell has declared:

"I wasn't actually convinced that the devil existed. But since I saw, in my mission, the most absurd and unmotivated violence among people who only a few months earlier had been living together peacefully; since I saw older people kill children by beating on their heads with a spade, well, since then, I do believe in the devil's existence."

"Time" magazine has reported on one of its covers another statement by a missionary: "Hell is devil-free now. They are all off duty in Rwanda".

Within each act of violence inflicted on a human being, there is something demoniac. Satan humiliates that image of God which is reproduced within each man. It is not possible that man, autonomously, considering the limited intelligence he has been provided with, may go to such extremes. Faith teaches us how to live through human events not on a merely human dimension, a dimension we can see and touch with our senses. We must read through reality in a theological and transcendent way, if we wish to perceive the most genuine depth of human events, while maintaining our capacity of being seized with astonishment, emotion, and a willingness to react. This is why, especially when forces overcoming man are at stake, praying is the very first aid we can and must offer to our oppressed brothers in Rwanda. Thy Kingdom come also to Rwanda, oh Lord!

Rwanda, following Bosnia, Somalia, Cambodia and Afghanistan, to a large extent once again disqualify the United Nations. This makes us become aware that there is neither a real authority controlling all Countries nor military headquarters capable to carry out those operations being agreed upon by the Security Council for the 'maintenance of peace' with the help of forces supplied by its members. The U.N. Chart provides for a General Staff, but because of the Soviet-American vie it has never been realized so far.

Today it must be given the highest priority among the international political issues. The world cannot just stand by as powerless witness to the suicide of one entire people, of many peoples, of the systematic extermination of one population by another.

In his two speeches to the FAO (5 December 1992) and the diplomatic Corps at the Holy See (16 January 1993), John Paul II clearly stated that the humanitarian right must prevail over and against the supremacy principle of a single Country.

"The real heart of international life - the Pope stated in his second speech - is Man, not Governments. We must acknowledge at this stage one of the most unquestionable and significant stages in the evolution of peoples' rights, which has been taking place during the XX century. The emerging individual stands as the basis of what we define as ëthe humanitarian rightí. There are some interests that go beyond Governments: these are the interests of human beings, and their rights. Yesterday as well as today. Man and his needs are still being threatened, alas, in spite of international correct writings, which are more o less binding, to the extent that a new concept has been dominating over the last months, the concept of "humanitarian interference" ... Once all the possibilities offered by diplomatic talks, the procedures being provided for by conventions, and international organizations have been enforced, and once, despite all of this, entire populations are going to be overcome by the attacks of some unfair aggressor, then Governments loose all rights to remain indifferent. Actually, their duty consists in disarming this aggressor, when any other means has proven to be inefficient ... The organization of society is only meaningful when it focuses on the individual, in a world made by man and for man."

These words are beautiful and most true. But we wonder: are we, the rich of this world, prepared to intervene as both the Pope and the U.N. are suggesting, to stop the Rwanda genocide? I dare say we are not.

The public opinion in our developed countries, the ordinary man are opposed to this.

Peoples' conscience, even when Christian, lacks a firm belief that the life of a man, of a people, is worth much more than money, domestic interests, or a quiet life. It is useless to wonder what we can do for Rwanda, when our conscience on solidarity at a worldwide level does not reach beyond the horizon of economic aid or, at most, the action of sending somebody to rescue a dozen or a hundred children. As long as our sensitivity stays unchanged, our upbringing stays unchanged, and the public opinion stays unchanged, issues will not change, not even at the summits of parliaments, governments, United Nations.

We often say that young people nowadays lack ideals. Life already gives them everything. They no longer have difficult and fascinating goals to attain, requiring hard work, as was the case for our generation who devoted itself to rebuild the Italian Nation destroyed by war and fascism, to create a democratic Country, to set in the economic development, welfare for all. Well, if this is so, international solidarity ought to be the "new frontier" where today's youth is to be directed. The establishment of a more correct and brotherly world, the cultural integration of different peoples, the struggle against hunger and underdevelopment; and, for communities and Christian families, the fascinating ideal of universal mission: these are the ideals into which young people should be educated so to nourish them with a motivation for life-worth, stimulating the enthusiasm to operate, which is necessary to set and attain vast goals in one's life. How far are we from this educational life-style, from these horizons of faith and of universal brotherhood and solidarity! We are far from this aim when it comes to our families, parishes, schools, youth association and groups, the catholic and lay press, or the TV palimpsests! How long are we going to go on without impressing a "missionary conscience" in the hearts of our people! It would be otherwise superfluous and useless to wonder "what we can do" for Rwanda!

JOURNAL DE L'ENFER

by Father Vito Misuraca

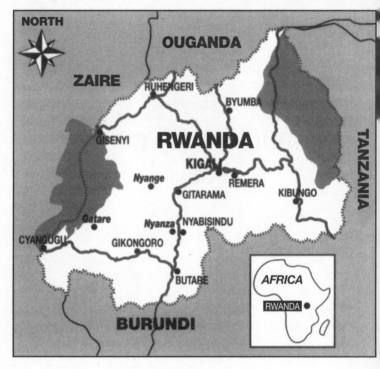

RWANDA

Small Rwanda (26.338 sqKms) is formed by a series of highlands with no outlet to the sea. The population is made up of 8 million people, 90% of them being Hutu, 9% Tutsi, and 1% Twas-Pygmy. In Kigali, the capital city, live 120,000 thousand people. Catholicism is the main religion (40%), while the rest of the population professes animism as well as other traditional beliefs. The per capita GNP is of USDols. 270, the main cash crop being coffee. Once part of the ex-Belgian Rwanda-Urundi colony, Rwanda became a republic in 1961, after having dismissed King Kigali V. In 1962 the country became independent. A new coup d'Ètat in 1973 gave the power to General Habyalimana, who legalized the regime with a referendum in 1978. The Rwanda Patriotic Front (Tutsi) in 1990 invaded the Country from Uganda, thus actually starting the present civil war between the Hutu and the Tutsi, which culminated in the crucial attack in February 1993 (which created one million refugees).

20

Kigali, 11 April

I have been in Kigali ever since the war broke out. I have come to spend a few days with the children, and to wish them a Happy Easter. I have called home, I have bought my airplane ticket, I am going back to Italy on 17/4/94. I will be visiting my relatives and will see Mom again.

I arrive on Tuesday, and I will be leaving on Wednesday before noon. I call the Papal Nuncio to tell him that I'd like to call in and say goodbye, but he is not there.

On Wednesday morning, a nun calls to tell me that the Nuncio has invited me for dinner. I accept and put off my departure to Thursday.

After dinner, we are chatting as we often do while serenely sipping our glasses of cognac. It's 8.30 p.m. April 6; suddenly we hear a first big explosion, then a second one, coming from the airport. I think I'd better go back to Remera, but if anything has happened over there, I might just as well stay at the Nuncio's residence.

From Remera*, the woman in charge assures me that everything is okay, they have not heard anything out there. I leave for Remera, and take the road passing by the CND**. This is a larger, smoother, and less dangerous road.

I am informed, over the phone, that the President

---

* Remera, where Father Vito's orphanage is situated, is 5 Kms away from the Kigali center.
** The CND is Rwanda parliament's seat.

and some other people have been killed. Nobody knows what's about to happen in the country. I think of what might happen, and how to save the children. There are many of them, and I actually do not know where to take them. The following morning, we are not allowed to leave the orphanage. All we can do is sit and wait for the situation to evolve. The Embassies do not disclose any information.

Little by little, we realize what the real situation is all about. Leaving with the children seems to be quite impossible. From our lodging, we can see many people being seized from their homes and slaughtered.

Some neighboring families reach us with their kids, telling us their incredible stories of how people injured by the bombs were then put to death with hoe blows.

This is what happened to a man whose family has found shelter by us.

All together, we are now 62 people, 36 of whom are children under 10 years of age.

These people rely on us, and I must rely on Providence.

We expect an evacuation but we have difficulties in contacting the outside. I succeed in communicating our situation.

Two soldiers arrive. They want to know who is living in this house. We tell them it is an orphanage, and show them the children. They are convinced and leave.

We keep waiting. We happen to be in an intermediate zone, and moving away with the children would be an impossible attempt as we would expose them to a certain death.

Here, trusting to Providence, we can eat and drink, while waiting for someone to come and give us the necessary help to move to a safer place.

We hope for a rescue by the U.N. and the Red Cross: we have already signalled our presence several times.

Remera, 12 April

The children are peaceful, mothers look after the cleaning, the house is always tidy, while praying helps us hope and stay confident.

Thinking of my father's sound faith, I prayed the Infant Jesus from Prague. I prayed the Tindari* Madonna , and to date, 12 April at 10.30 a.m., we are still here, waiting for and trusting God's Providence. We are following this absurd war personally: bombs are falling all around us, bullets are whizzing, and we are trapped. That's why we are still here.

Many soldiers from the opposing factions are lying in ambush along our street. If we go out, we risk to become either party's favorite target-shooting.

The U.N. are not coming, but even if they did,

---

* Tindari is a small town in the Messina province, Sicily, where a beautiful sanctuary to a Black Madonna has been established.

would I have enough courage to leave so many people? What will happen to them? My life has a goal if I can be of some help to somebody. I am a priest, and I have consecrated my life to God and to my fellow being. I don't know whether they will come and rescue us. Would it ever be possible?

The country has been put through fire and bloodshed. No place in Rwanda is safe.

If, by the grace of God, I overcome these difficult moments, it will be beautiful to go on working, even for this Kingdom of His.

I know that my relatives are worried, that they are most likely trying to have my news, but would it ever be possible to send news from the very center of the battle field? We hope that things will calm down in our neighborhood so to have some relief after five days* of bombing and ambushes, while we are right at the crossing of four military posts.

We hear people dying, we listen to the grenades flying over our heads, we witness the many houses being destroyed as well as the death of many innocent people. And we are still here, we are still alive by the grace of God.

Even the youngest children have understood the seriousness of the situation, and they are mainly the ones who give an example of wisdom, and are calm. Emma has proven to be a woman of great faith, the

---

* I began to write this war diary a few days after the fight started as we hoped that everything would settle quickly.

old Margherita, who takes care of Renzo and Josephine, is fine and busy as she looks after the two little scamps. Anastasia, our neighbor, is facing some difficulties with Marie Aimèe, her two-year old girl. Agata is a valuable help for Emma with the chore. Her whole family is here with us. For some time now, some calmness has fallen upon us, even if we can feel the close presence of soldiers. It's 12,40 p.m. of I don't know which day, we are tired of living in such a situation, everybody is running away, and we have been left behind with Providence.

I see that other young people have joined us, they are the guardians of some houses nearby. We are able to find some food and a place to sleep for them as well.

Until today, our two guardians Rutambi and Alberto have proven to have iron nerves and a lot of courage, but fatigue is beginning to show. The official radio broadcasting has toned down. On the contrary, the other* one is inciting to the massacre. Maybe, they will stop for a while, and then we will try to focus on the situation.

An unceasing fight has been going on all day long near our house.

This morning three Rwanda soldiers came and asked me how come we have not moved yet to some other place. I answered them that we did not have the possibility of leaving, and that I could not face

---

* The RTLM, free radio televion of the thousand hills.

the children with the danger of leaving on foot.

They have stayed near the house all day long, from where they are shooting.

As I know the radio propaganda of these days, I know that, if we leave on foot, the women will be slaughtered for the mere reason that they are Tutsi as well as the workers.

The children's behavior is astonishing, especially among the youngest ones: they stays indoors all day long, while waiting for the situation to become somewhat better: it is very hard.

I often thought of mom and of my brothers, today. I prayed for them, and I kept my father's photo in my hands, thus feeling encouraged. Whatever is going to happen, we will be together.

I feel deeply at peace within, I have tried whatever I could to reduce the discomforts of those who are living in our house, especially of the little ones. God has helped me solve this problem, and I hope that even in the future we will not loose our courage, but we will keep strong in our faith and hope.

I asked Emma if she was feeling serene, and she said she was calm and very confident.

The younger kids need some amusements, they need to go out but this is not possibile, as the military are back to shooting again. It's 5.25 p.m., the night will come soon. The Lord help us and the Tindari Madonna protect us!

I vowed to transform this house into a chapel to the Madonna and the divine mercy. I hope I will be able to fulfill my vow, if friends and benefactors who usually help me, will also help to carry it out while helping the children, as they have been doing so far. People struggle for money, and many of them who have always been in search of it now see their dreams coming to nothing. These are life-lessons one can never forget.

Food is being prepared, electricity is missing, and we must eat up what is left in the refrigerator. I'm thinking of all the people dying of hunger on the street or at home, while we have our daily food by the grace of God. Today we even have some meat and the Easter colomba* my brother Salvatore gave us.

A lot of people are at the mercy of bandits and lacking any help. Even worldwide organizations have left. A few individuals have stayed, but we are not in touch with one another. The situation in the country is not positive and, considering the massive negative propaganda, Belgians will never come back to Rwanda again.

I am concerned about the fact as I could not reassure my family that I am fine. We are now over sixty, both children and adults, and we encourage one another. I must encourage everybody: if I leave, they will be taken over by panic. How could I ever leave them on their own?

---

* The "colomba" is an Italian Easter-cake in the form of a dove.

I love these people, and they have always loved me.
They are like a family to me.

We can hear the U.N. forces passing by at a few
meters from us, but nobody comes to see us. God and
the Holy Lady are with us, and this is enough to us.

Remera, 13 April

A big fight broke out two hours ago. It's April
13, 1994. We don't know anything about what is
going on.

It's 7.30 a.m. Shooting has been reduced. We
must be informed on the actual situation: the entire city has become a battle-field. I could call the
guardians and have some tea prepared: if this lull
goes on for a while, we will be better.

We are on a zone being disputed by opposing factions, and I have a feeling that this is going to last
rather long. Hope is still our only friend, together with
faith. I am also sure that the Madon-na is protecting
this house, and each time I look at her image, I feel
encouraged and at peace. Bombar-dments have been
going on for seven days now, and we are still alive.

With the 15 bags of cement we had we have
reinforced a few side walls, especially where the
youngest kids are sleeping. The young people and
the men are sleeping in the hall, while the women
with babies to take care of have been placed in the
corridor; and the children are distributed in two

other rooms. I have my own room, where I try to put something down on paper.

We regularly clean the house in the morning and have managed to do it so far. We do feel like taking a shower today, but I don't know whether we have any water, as the conflict is raging and we can still hear threathening gun shots. Rifles and machine-guns are never at rest: they are fighting in Kimihurura and on the opposite hill. The cease-fire has been announced over the radio. Despite this, we can still hear some shooting: the gun shots are closer, it's 8 a.m. My antenna was hit by a bullet, and a bomb fell very close, right in our garden: two definitely fearful moments.

I am thinking of what it will be like when the war is over... misery, grief, hunger, retaliations. One can only hope that those hot tempers now causing so much bloodshed will calm down. This is the end of a long-lasting power, as well as of many compromises.

Because of these compromises, the Church is now paying the highest toll.

Churches have been transformed into real slaughter-houses, priests are being massacred, while refugees have their throats cut.

Several years of power and search for possession have come to an end over these last few days. I believe that, alongside the genocide of this people, we will have to remember the suffering and the death of many innocent people.

This is a lesson for everybody, most of all for all these military parades sent by the U.N. who should protect the innocent population instead of just watching as they did and as they are doing here.

In four months, the U.N. have spent one million dollars a day, without succeeding in stopping this people from being butchered.

I remember the words of Fatima's message: "At last, my spotless heart will overcome".

Last night we emptied the refrigerator, but the adults did not eat. We preferres to remain in our shelter and avoid making the least noise.

It was the right decision. Although we could not go out and buy something to eat for eight days, thanks to God, until now we haven't lacked anything. Water might have been a problem, but God did not allow us to go without it. As it often rained, we were able to collect a large supply of it. It is 8.15 a.m., and the struggle has shifted to another area of the city. Here, the birds are singing again. It is probably 'hot' on the other side of the city, but we fear and perceive the presence of soldiers in the ambush. This morning we did not do our chores as usual; we are experiencing difficult moments. We still manage to control our nerves.

We could still pray, so we remained in our corners, and children only had their tea at 9 o'clock. I was given a good cup of coffee and some of Anna's chestnuts together with many other treats she filled the parcels with, which she had sent to us. My brother Salvatore's parcel is also here: the candies he sent were often helpful to keep the children quiet.

The warbling of birds heartens us a little bit, we had become accustomed to the gun shooting, and now it has a totally different effect on us. Even Gasuku, our parrot, is singing. Our tiny little pet has turned out to be a good watchdog.

From time to time I think of Gatare* but I do not know anything about them over there. I wonder what is going on down in the South and what the nuns are doing. One can only hope that they have no problems.

Considering the news I have received, everything is to be done all over again, in all of the Rwanda dioceses. This will be the subject of another chapter.

It's 5.30 p.m., and I am back to writing. Everybody has left, and has forgotten us behind. You are the only One who is left to us, Lord, Your might and Your Providence are beyond of all human certainties. A priest must accept his life. Events develop in such a way that we couldn't do .anything else. We accept Your will, we surrender to it, with love and gratitude. You give us our life,

---

Gatare parish was founded by Father Vito Misuraca. It is situated in the Musebeya municipality (Gikongoro prefecture). The church was inaugurated on 20 August 1989, and the parish was established on 25 March 1992. Several activities were organized there such as the kindergarten, the primary school, catechism, dressmaking classes run by the Daughters of the Divine Zeal, specific classes for young people's training in different fields such as carpentry, soldering, masonry, plumbing, a brick workshop, a garage for car repairs, refresher courses for high-school kids. The structure has remained untouched although several components of the staff have been killed

and you take it away from us, there is absolutely nothing we can add. The human might, which has proven to be only death and destruction, at least during these days, is not able to grant any safety. It is only mere appearance and false certainty. Here, it's here that You intervene, oh Lord and Heavenly Father!

Men get armed to sow death, they crave for wealth and sow hate, while shattering justice in the belief they are actually building something, and yet they do not know that all this will eventually turn against themselves, and that they will become the victims of their own designs: we are witnessing this. First, they killed the Tutsi, then they killed the Hutu married to a Tutsi woman, then they killed whoever happened to be born in the South, and those who refused to accept their design to slaughter. Oh, Lord. You are the only one who can uphold us in these dreadful moments and give us the grace, according to your endless mercy and kindness.

Little Marie Aimèe cannot keep quiet when she has to. She wanted her mom to give her some cream. I told her off, explaining that I would buy a full carton of it. The girl is only two years old.

From time to time, some shooting reminds us of the war.

The children get ready for dinner, as everybody must be in bed by 6.30 p.m..

Another night is starting, the traps are many. We hope that everything will be okay. The Madonna of Tindari has extended her protection over this house.

Remera. 14 April

It's April 14, daybreak. From time to time you can hear some shooting coming from the posts nearby. We caní't figure out what's going on out there as the shots are faraway.

We are in an especially hot area, and there is nothing we can do about it. All you need to do is poke your nose out of the door, and you are machine-gunned. God is with us, and with these little innocent children of His.

It's 9.30 a.m., we have already said our morning prayers. The passage of the Gospel I read is about Jesus blessing children. It came natural to me to say that love is the only valuable thing, while those people who spend their whole lifetimes accumulating material goods, all of a sudden might lose everything they have. This is what we are learning these days.

It's 10.30 a.m. They are shooting close to the house: we are going through ten difficult minutes. Bullets whiz from all sides. We are sure that our house is being protected, while we are being surrounded by one single battle-field. Children are quietly sitting in the hall. It's 10.55 a.m., and it's raining. This is a real blessing for us and for everybody: the air is purified, and we can add at least some water to our supply. We have been using our neighbours' tanks for eight days already, while they have been taken shelter with us.

Housecleaning is guaranteed, bathrooms included. The house is tidy, and even the youngest ones have understood they must be very careful how they behave and never scream.

It's 2.50 p.m. The day is especially calm, if one can ever say so. We are always expecting to hear that they have found a solution, and that we can go out. But gun shooting is a never ending thunder.

Among the men present here we wonder if we can work out a solution to leave.

Our hill lays between two fires: we can only trust in God opening up a passage for us. We have been protected until now, and I am confident that we will overcome this situation uninjured. If we leave, what are we going to eat? What are we going to drink?

Where will we end up?

We hope that the tempers will calm down, and that life will smile again. While the city was being put to fire and was undergoing the bloodshed, we were living on this oasis of hope and confidence.

Remera, 15 April

15 April 1994: some people arrived during the night. We don't know them. From 2 to 3 o'clock in the morning, a big battle was going on. They threw some grenades very close to our house, and even shot against the windows, we went through moments of real terror. Then the battle was over, and the soldiers

left. Nobody was injured, but we must take a radical decision. We take stock of the situation. We check the three cars are running properly, one of which tends to overheat, unfortunately. We talk to the soldiers in the nearby post who tell us to leave, if we have any chance. That's our intention.

The people present here are as follows: Father Vito Misuraca, in charge of the orphans of Remera Kigali; women: Emma Mujawabikira, Agata Rukemampunzi, Margherita Kankindi, Anastasia Nyiramana, Theresa Mukantabana, Edith Karebwire, Anastasia Nikomeze.

Men: Vianneyi Rumanyika, Theonesti Hakizimana, Albert Hanyuliryayo, Agustini Munyankusi, Gasimba Frodualdi, Athanasi Munyentamati, Vedasti Halinditwali, Alphonsi Maniragaba, Antoni Kagaba, Feliciani Gatabazi, Camilli Uwimana.

Young men and women and teen-agers: Thierry Nyilimana, 16 years old, Charlotte Mukagahutu, 17, Vincenti Karasira, 24, Callisti Senyoni, 22, Oliva Nyilimana, 19, Bertilla Hakizimana, 17, Maria Letizia Uwitonze, 16, Jean-Paul Shingiro, 15, Regina Nyiraneza, 14, Mwizerwa, 16, Annonciata Uwimana, 17, Marie-Claire Mukatuza, 17.

Children: Nakure, 12, Carine Nyilimana, 12, Athanasiya Nyirandenzaho, 12, Dèsirè Mazimpaka Fidel, 12, Bosco Twagirimana, 12, Fortunata Nyiranzeyimana, 11, Venusti Twizeyimana, 8, Cecile Mukamazimpaka, 9, AngÈlique Mushimyihimana, 9, Victori Nungubuhe, 8, Delphine Kamariza, 8,

Edwardi Habarurema, 8, Berthleem Nizeyimana, 5, Bertrand Dukundane, 6, Nadëge Uwase, 6, Donati Nzabimana, 6, Protogëne Ndayindurwa, 6, Theogeni Nsekanabanga, 3, Wilma Uhorakeye, 5, Marcel Niyonsaba, 4, Marie-Lucie Mukeshimana, 2, Renzo Nsanzumuhire, 2, Josèphine Mukeshimana, 2, Lilly Habijuru, 1, Jaul Niyigema, 6 months.

Thierry Nyilimana, Agustini Munyankusi, Gasimba Frodualdi, Athanasi Munyentamati, Vedasti Halinditwali, Alphonsi Maniragaba, and Feliciani Gatabazi stayed in Kigali as there was not enough room for everybody. We are determined to come back and pick them up. To do otherwise would mean certain death for everybody.

We don't hear of them again.

As soon as we reached the paved road, we realized that there was no way out. Only a miracle could save us: 12 or 14 year old boys under adults' orders are killing as many Tutsi as they can. This is the beginning of a whole series of troubles for us: Emma tells them a story about when we were attacked by their enemies, who wanted to steal the orphans' food. They all have mercy, and ask me if I am Belgian. If that were the case, I wouldn't have much time left to live. Every other ten meters, different groups ask for the same thing: they all want money. At the Kigali rond-point, the situation becomes even harder. A soldier is looking for Tutsi people as a furious dog, and this is when one of our boys, Camilli Uwimana, 28 years old, is made to step off: then two teen-agers are ordered to stab him to death.

We continue with broken hearts; many of us had a knife placed at our throats. I speak Kinyarwanda* and make them laugh a little, and so we go on. It takes four hours to drive a little more than 5 kms. Thank God, we meet a soldier who knows me, who escorts us to the Nyabarongo river, and who give us the custody of two other children, whom I welcome with the others. Kigali is a hell bedlam. Everybody does whatever they feel like.

Many soldiers, thank God, try to help passers-by, while others take advantage of the situation, to steal as much as they can.

Chaos is order compared to the Kigali bedlam.

Kigali is the kingdom of death, where people are killed with no mercy, where all respect for life has vanished. But we have been saved, by the grace of God. All our children are safe as well as many adults.

Once we got across the Nyabarongo river, we had to leave our Renault. I have no regrets: what mattered was the life of the many people I could save. At the city outskirts, we depart from a group of people, and continue towards Ruhango with the two cars.

We stop in Gitirama to get freshened up at least a little; I'm craving for a drink, sweating as I am all

---

* A local language.

over, but I am happy. In Ruhango, Father Stany welcomes us and gives us all that he can. Most of all, he offers us a shelter where to spend the night. It's our first quiet night after many dangerous days and the terrible flight from Kigali.

Finally, everybody can take a shower and rest for a while!

The sub-prefect of Ruhango let me have 40 liters of Mazout. He is nice to us, giving advice and updating us on the situation.

Nyanza, 16 April

On Saturday 16 April, I send the car in Butare to collect news and despatch a message to Nayanza, Father Eros welcomes us at his orphanage (directed and run by the Rogation Fathers), and two families who have been staying with us so far succeed in joining their relatives. Here, in Nyanza, we are all together 44; we feel much safer and pray a lot to live better days ahead.

Nyanza, 17 April

This is not an inter-ethnical war. Rather, it is the application of a devilish planned design.

Over 30 priests are either missing or dead. About ten nun communities have been wiped out. Until now, 13 parishes have been destroyed with all their human content.

Nothing and nobody was spared. More than 7500 people were killed in Kibeho, and the church is still burning. When man loses his reason, then absurdity becomes his only face value.

List of the children and adults living at the orphanage with Father Vito Misuraca.
1. Josèphine Mukeshimana, 2 yrs old
2. Renzo Nsanzumuhire, 2 yrs old
3. Marie-Lucie Uwambajimana, 2 yrs old
4. Silvestri Nkundimana, 2 yrs old
5. Lilly Habijuru, 1 yr old
6. Beda Mushimiyimana, 3 yrs old
7. Theogeni Nsekanabanga, 3 yrs old
8. Emmanueli Mugabo, 3 yrs old
9. Alexi Maniragaba, 4 yrs old
10. Marcel Niyonsaba, 4 yrs old
11. Wilma Uhorakeye, 5 yrs old
12. Protogëne Ndahindurwa, 6 yrs old
13. Maria Mukakalisa, 6 yrs old
    died on 15/5/1994
14. Justine Ujeneza, 6 yrs old
15. Donati Nzabimana, 6 yrs old
16. Serge Mukiza, 7 yrs old
17. Victori Nungubuhe, 8 yrs old
18. Venusti Twizeyimana, 8 yrs old
19. Delphine Kamariza, 8 yrs old
20. Angèlique Mushimyihimana, 9 yrs old
21. Edwardi Habarurema, 9 yrs old
22. Fortunata Nyiranzeyimana, 11 yrs old
23. Carine Nyilimana, 12 yrs old

24. Athanasiya Nyirandenzaho, 12 yrs old
25. Bosco Twagirimana, 12 yrs old
26. Toto Mwizerwa, 16 yrs old
27. Mukatuza Marie-Claire, 17 yrs old
28. Annonciata Uwimana, 17 yrs old
29. Olive Nyilimana, 17 yrs old
30. Charlotte Mukagahutu, 17 yrs old

The adults:
1. Emma Mujawabikira
2. Edith Karebwayire
3. Theresa Mukantabana
4. Margarita Kankindi
5. Callixte Senyoni
6. Vincenti Karasira
7. Albert Hanyuliryayo
8. Antoine Kagaba

Nyanza, 18 April

We have been in Nyanza since 16 April, Father Eros has welcomed us and has done all he could so that we would be lacking anything. After the first two days spent recovering a little bit, we have begun to make ourselves available for the house chores. Rutambi and Albert help in the kitchen. Vicenti and Senyoni are working as guardians. Oliva is incharge of setting the table. Women do as much as they can to help in the house. Life here is going on peacefully. The children have attended mass at the parish. They have been making friends locally and are well integrated.

I talked with the Fathers in Mugombwa over the phone. Everything is fine up till now, Monday 18 April 1994, although one fears something bad is about to happen. Some bad news is coming in: Mugombwa has been attacked. The church has become the graveyard for many people. Fathers and nuns are leaving, they are directed to Butare; because they have not experienced the sad days of Kigali directly, they are now faced with a terrible shock.

On Wednesday, tragedy falls on Butare. Many civilians lose their lives. All those who had shown some dislike for the regime have been slaughtered with no mercy whatsoever. The Tutsi have been decimated. None of them have the slightest chance of escaping. Gikongoro has been attacked. They are fighting inside of the refugee camps. Everybody has been slaughtered: estimates account for thousands of people. Even within the parish there have been some innocent victims. Cyanika is razed to the ground. Refugees have been killed inside the church. We have no news about the priests. Churches and religious institutions are part of the target, with no respect at all.

Nyanza, 22 April

Today, 22 April, is Nyabisindu turn. I do not know how the whole thing will end. For sure, hun-

41

dreds of people have already lost their lives. One can see trucks passing by, packed with young people going God knows where. Considering yesterday's operation throughout the town, it isnít difficult to imagine that they are being sent to the front* by hook or by crook.

Now we hear the shooting again but we do not know actually what's going on. A police officer came to announce they would be coming to inspect and that we should not worry about the orphanage.

We prepared the list of all those present, and I have also prepared the working papers for those arriving from Kigali. We kept all the boys at home, only letting them come down for dinner.

All around us, houses are on fire. You can hear people screaming. Rifles never tone down.

The Fathers from the parish have found shelter here. They are going through moments of terror. Our neighbours sent in their children, whom we inserted in our lists.

---

* *When the tragic events of April 1994 broke out, the military Front was settled at the Byumba prefecture as well as in several municipalities of the Ruhengeri prefecture. A military detachment of the Rwanda Popular Front settled in Kigali at the CND (seat of Rwanda parliament), according to the Arusha agreements. This detachment opposed a fierce resistance, thus enabling many people to reach safer areas, away from the Presidential Guard, the Interahamwe and all of those who had joined them for a methodical killing of all the Tutsi, be they men, women or children, as well as all their political opponents. Many civilians fled from their homes, taking shelter in the churches or wherever they felt safe, as had happened years before when other violent episodes had upset the country. At that time, those who took refuge in the churches were spared. This time, the Hutu, being incited by RTLM (Free Radio Television of Thousand Hills) inviting to kill "all the Enemies", did not respect anything or anybody. Nor even the churches, such as the one in Nyanza, for example, which they completely razed to the ground, thus burying people inside it under the debris.*

42

For sure, they will never see their parents again. The night passes by quite peacefully.

Nyanza, 23 April

This morning I have learnt that the refugee camp in Kaduha has been destroyed.

Over 10 thousand people were there and no one has survived. All refugee camps have been decimated. Reliable sources inform us that over 25 thousand people died in less than three days only in the camps of Cyanika, Murambi, Kibeho, Kaduha, Mugombwa.

The military action in Butare resulted in over 30 thousand deaths; the city is paying a high price. Wherever you have a massive gathering of people, if soldiers do not arrive first, then armed gangs come and destroy everything. All of the institutions have been destroyed, while cadres of opposing ethnical groups have all killed. Only a few of them managed to escape. All the officers belonging to the opposition have been exterminated together with their families. The Hutu cruelty has wiped out entire families in any single municipality. If it is true that Tutsi were 9% of the population (but they were 23 or 24%, as far as I know), more than half a million of people have died only for the ethnical issue. But how many of them have died for the political issue? Which balance do we have on the front?

When we speak of hundreds of thousands of people, we are only referring to the innocent population who had nothing to do with war. This was not a purely ethnical war, as they want us to believe, this was an organized plan, prepared and carried out with cold determination.

Only a few Europeans have now been left in the entire Butare and Gikongoro regions. Everything is destroyed: institutions, schools, hospitals, social services, parishes, nutritional centers, and so on. Who will meet the needs of those who are staying behind?

Many educated Rwandan people were killed because tehy belonged either to the Tutsi race or to the opposition. Priests were decimated, dealers were killed, nuns were slaughtered, teachers are no longer there, mayors and councillors disagreeing over their responsibilities for the carnage have disappeared, prefects keeping to the order have been dismissed, but where are they now? Quite a few decades of history have been cancelled by the devilish fury of a handful of gangsters who demand the respect and the submission on the part of an entire people, without understanding that all that is going on now will have fatal consequences in the near future.

All around here, everything is still on fire. The radio is changing its way of speaking.

It may be because the military forces are running wild. They start asking for help and inviting people to avoid slaughtering. But who on earth is still listening to them?

44

Things will end up as in Kigali. Those who stole first, had been robbed by those who came later on, and now gangs and factions are fighting one another. They compete as those who kill the most, and then boast of their bravadoes.

Nyanza, 23 April

Today the Bishop called me on the phone. He hasn't realized yet that the old institutions of the Church are by now obsolete. Their function is over. They haven't spoken up until now, they haven't spent a word in favour of their own priests, they have hid themselves, they never intervened. The death of so many priests and nuns must cause us to ponder and appreciate how much man needs true moral values, instead of only material things. Evangelization, as it has been carried out here so far, and the administration of sacraments ought to be the outcome of a cate-chesis which is not merely verbal, but the result of a social and public commitment instead.

On the contrary, the Church has to stay outside of any political compromise. Bishops and priests had been granted some privileges from the former regime until now: they obtained benefits, they exchanged favours, but the Church also registered blows under the belt by government officers.

Too many compromises with the civil power, too many connections between the civil power and the Church authorities, too many lies. All of this is being paid today with the blood of most of the Tutsi priests and many Hutu priests, with the destruction of virtually all the structures of the Church, including the parishes and presbyters as well.

6 o'clock p.m. Claudine Nyiraneza, a seven year old girl, arrives at the Nyanza orphanage. She has walked for about 30 kms or maybe more, her right foot has been injured after been hit by a machete, she leans on a stick. Her family has been killed, and she hasn't been eating for days. We hope that others will be able to make it here, as she has, thus escaping the massacre. We put her up as well as possible, we feed her a little, and we give her some medical treatment. Her slash is very bad, but it will heal. She is terrified. Maybe she will tell us her story tomorrow.

I have just been given confirmation this night to my fears: in Kaduha people have been killed practically everywhere, the church is packed with corpses, but they have not put it on fire. More than ten thousand refugees were sheltering in it, according to the last estimates being confirmed by several witnesses.

Death squads and common criminals, led by government soldiers, and with the prefects' full agreement, are destroying the country; they pour fuel in the houses before setting them on fire. One can often see people running away, not being used to theshooting: adults, old people, children, women. Everybody tries to find some shelter, while soldiers are playing their target-shooting. Then, government trucks arrive to burgle the houses; they steal, pour fuel over the floor, and set it on fire.

One wonders: who is the enemy really?

You can often see enormous fires stretching out and burning crops, woods, and houses. I canít believe that fire can figure out any ethnical diffe-rences. This is not limited to a genocide, it is also an ecocide. Itís something which they had prepared with a devilish character, something that only an unsound mind could ever conceive. It is a craving for power, and the presumption that one can actually be the master of somebody else's life, that one can dispose of the life of others, and believing that all of this misbehaviour will remain unpuni-shed. In a war you have armed soldiers, but here you have babies a few months old being ripped up, mothers trying to protect their children being mas-sacred with the strokes of a hammer, a hatchet, a machete or of stones. Here you have helpless old people who are beated and kicked before having their throats cut, adults who are maimed in any part of their bodies before being killed, while the luckier ones, if one can ever say so, are put to death with a gun shot aimed at their heads.

Nyanza, 24 April

It's Sunday. We say Mass with all the young people here at the orphanage. Nobody is in the parish. The Christian population does not go to mass: if the few people left started walking on the street, they would most likely be subject to tortures; they might even be killed if they belong to the other race.

From time to time you can hear some shooting around here, then we realize that a few shots had been saved for some cows. Now they are sharing out the meat.

It's pouring down, which will prevent them form hunting the Tutsi - at least for a while.

It's 3.30 p.m. We learn the sad news that Father Mattaio Ngirumpatse has died. Two Benebikira nuns have also been killed together with all the people who had taken shelter at their place. There are two versions regarding the Father's death.

It's 4.00 p.m. A group of people armed with sticks approaches our fence. Father Eros speaks to them, and they leave, at last. Our boys, having overheard the oncversation, refer that they intend to attack us tonight at eight o'clock.

These are terrible moments. Our life is hanging by a thread. We call the police station, looking for help and explaining our concern.

The post captain comes together with some other officers to grant us their protection. We hear people screaming, gunshots all night long, and we fear the worst.

The next morning, they advise us to place the older boys of the orphanage all around the fence.

They are all armed with iron bars, stones and sticks. The police station commander keeps in touch with us.

This is not a war carried out by soldiers anymore. This is a war between armed gangs wanting to rob, kill, and sack. The situation has slipped out of the hands of the very people who had planned this carnage.

They say that some soldiers, and even officers, after being informed that their loved once had been savagely murdered, have revolted, and are now slaughtering the Hutu ethnical group in revenge. Many of those who have been killing over these last days, are getting into panic now. The country is governed by the rule of the strongest, in the midst of the most complete insecurity.

In Burundi the situation in not that good either. We hope that the convoy which left a few days ago has reached its destination in Europe.

People are now saying: "Imana ikinze amaboko" (literally: God closed his hands, meaning that God did not allow the orphanage to be touched).

Every night we can see our neighbour's houses on fire. The hills all around are covered with fires. People are destroying the houses of those who have been killed, and rob their property. It's terrible to see how naturally they commit certain crimes.

There is a police barrier close to the orphanage entry, and every day since the slaughtering broke out, here, in Nyanza, people are been killed and thrown into a ditch over twenty meters deep. Women are stripped and maimed, mothers trying to save their children have their arms cut with hatchet strokes, lances run through tortured bodies, and, knives finish them off. Most people are killed with hammer strokes and thrown into the ditch while they are still alive. This is the case of a Benebikira nun from the Nyanza community who had been thrown half-alive in a ditch and who only died after two days down there.

Children arriving to the orphanage are in dread. They tell us incredible stories and unbelievable atrocities.

Nyanza, 25 April

The night passes by quite peacefully. Two policemen arrived yesterday evening at 6.30, and took up service alongside our guardians for security reasons.

Their presence comforts us, although we have to be extremely careful they do not discover the three priests we are hiding: it would be a disaster if they did.

They are a parish priest, a curate and a priest from Gikongoro; they are looking for them because of their Tutsi origin; they took shelter with us trying to escape from death.

Our guardians have proved to be reliable so far, and our children do not say a word to anybody outside. We hope that we will all be able to survive this useless carnage.

Nyanza, 26 April

Kigali has been cannonaded during the night. We can hear the rumble, for a radius of 50 kms as the crow flies. At 6 o'clock this morning, we drove the policemen to their station.

The radio is broadcasting a bulletin for the death squads; maybe life can start again little by little.

The market is likely to be overflowing with various stuff on sale, as people from the surroundings have robbed the houses of those whom they have killed. Their only concern is to accumulate as much as they can, and this is somehow providential, as their attention is this way diverted from the Tutsi hunt to the robberies.

Our boys are 'on the steps' near the orphanage, and nothing escapes their notice.

We found out how to make them feel important as they couldn't stand staying inside any more. Little by little they put together a great story on cowboys in the Far West.

Girls are in charge of the water supply and the cleaning, and the house is kept tidy.

Armed gangs seem to have disappeared, while only a few passers-by walk down the street.

We are informed that the great blood-thirst is over in Butare; people are now looking for humanitarian aid. And this is now the starting of the big tragedy of hunger, disease, daily life in a country which has succeeded in destroying itself over just a few days.

The night was quiet. Our boys are alert. All around us, tempers are calming down, people are back to their normal behaviours. We wonder when life will actually start again, when we will be able to go out, take stock of the situation, and understand how things are developing.

We receive some news from the outside: a market is being organized in Butare three days a week, but outside the city.

Some stores are re-opening, but not all of them. People are still afraid.

Here, in Nyanza, stores are being looted. It's a good occasion for poor people to become rich for a few days. Money has depreciated by 100%: a pack of cigarettes which used to cost 90 Rwf is now 200 Rwf. You can't find any other articles. Today we could have a bottle of beer on the table. It's an event which we celebrate!

We are informed that terrible things are happening in Kigali, fighting is going wild, casualties are destined to die, and they already speak of epidemics because of the manycorpses left unburied.

According to some information spreading around there are about 3500 corpses inside the Mugombwa Church alone; one week has gone by, and they are still unburied.

All around the parish building, only pieces of the wall in ruins have been left standing.

In Cyanika, there are more than 4,000 unburied

corpses left inside the church. The Parish priest was killed right in the middle of the Dispensary.

In Kaduha, there are more than 10,000 corpses inside the church, at the hospital and in the parish house.

In Murambi, there are still unburied corpses lying inside the church.

In Mushubi, the parish house has become the graveyard for many people. We don't know the exact number of corpses.

In Kibeho, there are 7.500 people or more, inside the church alone. The church has been destroyed, corpses have been partially burnt. Other parishes have undergone the same fate: Muganza, Gisagara, Simbi, Nyamiyaga, Ngoma, Karama, Kiruhura, Cyahinda, Nyumba, etc. This piece of news, and many others ones even more tragic, cause us to shudder.

Nyanza, 28 April

It's 4 o'clock p.m. Two soldiers arrive on a jeep taking fourteen boys and girls to us: three of them are injured on their heads and legs. We welcome them and try to give them first aid treatments. Our family is widening out, including three fourteen year old girls and children ranging from three to nine years of age. The soldiers are accompanied by a Mwenebikira nun from the Nyanza community: she is the one who gathered the children.

They are: Ancilla Uwamahoro, 16 yrs old, originally from Kigali, seriously wounded on the head.

Gisële Dushime, 5, and Anne Paulette Umutoni, 7: these are two sisters coming from Kigali.

Rosine Kayirangwa Hergan, 5, and her brother Davide Kayigumire, 12, from Kigali.

Ange Petit, 5, and her brother Tantan Martin, 4, whose father was working with the disabled in Nyanza.

Sabine Kampire, 6, and Harmel Muhimpundu, 4, two sisters originally from Gikongoro, and residing in Kigali.

Oda and Odile Rutagengwa, twin sisters, 14 years old, coming from Kigali. One of them is wounded on the head with a lance stroke. Cirille Umurerwa, 13, Nyanza. J.M.

Vianneyi Mazimpaka, 9, from Rusatira. Oliva Muzayiruwa, 17, from Rusatira, shows five machete injuries on her head, while a lance stroke in her calf has pierced through her leg.

At 5.30 p.m., another six year old boy arrives. He is from Nyanza, he has lost his parents, all his brothers and his sisters.

Nyanza, 29 April

The slaughtering goes on in the inner part of the country, and the escalation of violence doesn't appear to slow down. On the radio, just words: they are happy because the Belgian government has refused a visa to one of the would-be ministers responsible for the genocide and the Rwanda tragedy. Children keep on coming in, and telling incredible stories, which are sadly true.

The presidential Guard and the Interahamwe are not on the front: they continue to massacre civilians. As a matter of fact, many soldiers still on the front ignore that their families have been slaughtered with the blows of a hammer or a hatchet. The mayors who opposed the massacres have been killed. Many soldiers as well as many policemen joined the gangs of murderers, while many people actively participated in the events, in the belief that they were saving the Country. Now, they say that if both the Interahamwe and the soldiers leave, peace will be back. Now, they realize that what they did was an enormous mistake, while disease is breaking out, and the big Rwanda tragedy is just at its very beginning. This is going to be the tragedy of Central Africa, for sure.

I listened to the spoken newspaper of France, which mentioned Cyangugu, and the 5,000 refugees who were attacked, a large number of which succeeded in fleeing to Zaire.

But they still haven't heard of the massacres in the communities of Nchili, Nyakizu, Muganza, Runyinya, Kivu, Rwamiko, Gishanvu, Kinyamakara, Musange, Kaduha, Muko, Karama.

I am only referring to those massacres the witnesses agree upon, where entire refugee camps have been exterminated: they weren't just 5,000 people, but more, many more.

The only thing which is left to us, is the hope that those children we are welcoming, will smile again while living among the others, although their eyes will be filled with endless sadness.

Tonight, Father Eros and I have been trying to call the entire world, but the phone lines were always engaged. We took courage again, thinking that they were probably busy trying to help us.

We bought a cow; we hadn't had any meat for about a month. We will have some tomorrow, and the day after tomorrow. Children are happy for this, and so are we. We thank Providence because we never run out of our daily bread nor of health.

We are exhausted, but happy. Our sacerdotal action has been useful to save several human lives, at least. At the very bottom of our hearts, we hope to see our families again and our country, but, here, we are cut off from the world.

Nyanza, 30 April

This morning, I drove the three policemen back. I had the possibility of seeing what the city looked like, and the spots where the atrocities were being committed. Everything looks depressing: fear and shame are written all over the people's faces. They start to lack everything, hunger is increasing, and many people wonder what they will ever be able to buy with the little money they've got left.

Inflation has increased even today, cigarettes are now 400 Rwf per pack. Tomorrow it's going to be even worse.

We understand from the radio that the responsible agents of these atrocities are beginning to be less cruel; they are realizing the mistake they have made; they are starting to realize that they had miscalculated, and are now desperately searching for some international help, but fortunately nobody is paying attention to them.

What are they going to offer to people if no activity can be resumed? Nobody is going back to work, as the salary arrears were never paid. Moreover, as salaries have not been updated, one would need to work one week to purchase two pounds of rice.

I have been informed that the Nyanza councillor, responsible for the death of many people, has been coolly stabbed and cut at his throat in his house.

The executors were the same people who had slaughtered others together with him.

History repeats itself. The trouble is that we never learn.

All the children who joined the orphanage between yesterday and today are less than 10 years old. There are their names:

Jean-Marie Vianneyi Shyaka, from Nyanza.

Jean-Paul Mugabo, from Nyanza.

Innocenti Kayisire, from Nyanza.

Nkurunziza, coming from Masango, a town 35 kms away.

Oreste Gatete, from Nyanza.

Masabo, from Ruhashya, a nearby town.

Dieu Donnè Gatari, from Nyanza.
Ntabwoba, from the town of Musange.
Mushimyihimana Gikongoro, from Masango.
Justin Mukomana, from Masango.
Twishimire, from Muko, a town 40 Kms away.
Claudin Nyiraneza, from the prefecture of Gikongoro.
Jean-Luc Kinigi, from Nyanza.
Placide Toto, from Nyanza.
Akizanye ?
Marie-AimÈe Umubyeyi, from Rwesero.
Marie-Ange Mizero, from Rwesero.

Nyanza, 1 May

Another day has gone by, the weather is fine but our problems are increasing.

We have been able to keep the situation under control at the orphanage until now. In the afternoon, we have taken a few hours of rest as it often happens that we are woken up by one problem or other.

Someone is knocking at my door: I wake up with a start: it's 3.00 p.m. I open the door, and to my great joy I see Consul Costa who has come to visit us. We don't have too much time, but we take the opportunity of exchanging some news.

In Italy, there are many people willing to help us leave this place safe and sound.

Someone might come to rescue us, but the big

problem is that several barriers have been set all along the roads, and there are still some bloodthirsty people who may kill without mercy only to please their chiefs. I was told that they receive 500 Rwf - something more than a dollar - for each person they kill. Our only prospect is to evacuate our children by helicopter: a gigantic operation! At any rate, we made our decision: either we leave with all the children and the personnel or we stay with them. To leave alone wouldn't make any sense. There is no reason for leaving now, after having undergone so many sacrifices to protect all these unfortunate innocent people. Some of our children are hunted, so we found a new identity for each one of them, and if they were to come and check our lists, they wouldn't find anybody. The Consul promises to come again within a few days, and we will entrust him with our newsletters to be sent to Italy.

The Consul has some trouble with his car. I give him my jeep: it was the last vehicle I had, so now I really have to go on foot!

Being a bit encouraged, we celebrate the evening with some lemon water and a new confidence in our hearts. One more reason to hope!

Nyanza, 4 May

It's 5.00 p.m. Some soldiers arrive to inspect the orphanage. Children are ordered to go to their rooms, while policemen and representatives of the

Presidential Guard inspect the toilets, the galleries, the dining room, the ceilings and our rooms. As they pass where the children are, they try to gather information on their origins, their identities, the reason why they are at the orphanage. They pretend to be uninterested, but they actually examine everything very carefully, especially under the beds and in the closets. Two soldiers were left outside to check that nobody left.

In the end, they inspect the chapel and the nearby building, where the three priests have been hiding for several days now. They question them, and force them to collect their belongings and follow them, while telling them that the orphanage is not a safe place for them.

They make them step into their jeep and leave to Gitwe. I realize that there is nothing else we can do for them. As it gets dark, I feel overwhelmed by the deepest sorrow. I quiver with horror and anger, wondering why there is so much absurdity, so much crazy folly.

Nyanza, 5 May

Here I am, back to my notes again. This war we have been going on for a month tomorrow, and we are still living in the greatest insecurity.

Yesterday, at 5.00 p.m., some soldiers came and inspected the orphanage once again. I am still thinking of the three priests who were killed. That news has cut deep inside of me. Life, here, isn't really worth anything anymore, and the more time goes by, the more problems we have to face up to.

Children keep coming in, asking to be put up: Over one hundred of them in three days.

What shall we do? All around us there is only material and moral poverty. We strive to resist, to control that tension blocking our muscles. Everyday we are informed of and hear about new horrors, which make us shudder.

From the radio they keep on repeating that peace is back, but, here, the slaughtering has never ceased. The worst is that they broadcast religious songs, which we can't stand any more as they have become odious, if one considers their context.

Yesterday, the orphanage in Gisenyi was completely evacuated. We hope to be evacuated too, as soon as possible. We hope somebody will manage to avoid another tragedy taking place here, too.

We have been looking for the Italian Consul already since yesterday. He called us and said that he was coming today. We are waiting for him, at least to entrust him with our mail to our families in Italy. I am sure that the lack of news on our part makes them suffer over there.

If only we had a camp phone, communications would be much easier. Only now do we realize that these are essential things in Third World Countries. I would add, even more basic than transportation means, no matter how badly we miss the latter.

Father Eros and Emma have some stomach problems, and they are not feeling too well. We are lacking proper medications, we do not have any doctors, nervous tension is very high and we are beginning to run out of energy. Maybe they are just beginning to debate these issues about the rights, duties, circumstances and procedures or to negotiate how to save some innocent children. Time goes by and everything becomes increasingly tragic to us! The situation is coming to a head, and insanity is becoming a wholesale issue. We are sure that all the negotiations being carried out faraway from the conflicts can only minimally solve the problem if at all; on the contrary, they do underline the issues, as the interests at stake are too many and a lot of people, occasionally of good will, are there to blow on the fire. Something like the "televised humanitarian agencies", or better, the "occasional phantom agencies", which arrive right on the conflict spot only to be interviewed and shown on a television screen. Some of these embezzled the help destined to the Rwandan population in distress, then left again without doing anything. May God help us. He is our only real hope!

At the orphanage, we have added some tables from the dining hall, and many children are sleeping on them, two by two. We lack mattresses; we don't have enough dishes; we asked somebody to supply us with what is necessary but it seems they have real transportation problems. We still don't know whether this can be arranged, but we do hope in a positive solution.

A trader from Butare came at 3.00 p.m. with a limited amount of blankets, dishes, spoons and even beverages. We were really left short of everything. At least, we have solved some practical problems for tomorrow. He promised he would send some rice, beans and potatoes as soon as he could; all we need is to find a military escort.

We have been informed that six priests were arrested in Gikongoro in two days, and that they fell into the gendarmery's hands or, more likely, they were killed.

This is a political issue: even if the two ethnic clans were to come to an agreement, I really don't see how they would ever be able to live together. Those who saw their parents, their brothers, their sisters being killed for no reason at all will never forget. The Church will have to start all over again, taking care of solving concrete problems first, the first one being that of facilities, which no longer exist. Many priests and bishops of the local regular clergy never declared their opinion on anything; how could they ever be given charge of the future reconciliation and reconstruction of this Country?

Many congregations have been decimated; seminaries do not exist any more; many teachers have been killed. A large part of the population has actively participated in the massacres, especially young people. When they speak of a helpless population in Kigali on the radio, we actually don't know whom they are referring to, considering that most people have now joined the armed militia. In the South of the Country helpless people have been decimated without a reason.

Nyanza, 6 May

Today is especially cold and rainy. One would say that the sky is somehow participating in the sorrow of this innocent people. The war has been going on for a month already. We will never forget these moments for their brutality, hate, the innocent bloodshed, as well as for the absurdity of the whole situation. There is no point in trying to find the proper words to describe these events as they go beyond human reason. Animals would never sink so low.

I believe we will never speak again of the Country of the thousand hills, while we will refer to the Country of the thousand horrors and infamies, where the monster replaces man, where reason is totally absent and the logic of cruelty and bloodshed prevails.

Nyanza, 8 May

It's a sunny Sunday. The number of children has doubled in a few days' time. The staff is not as yet accustomed to the special times we are living in, and they do not realize that feeding all these people for the weeks ahead is becoming a problematic issue.

We informed the Diocese, but I'm afraid that the situation is as difficult over there.

Most of the parishes have been destroyed, becoming the graveyard of tens of thousands of people. We still don't know the number of priests and nuns put to death or buried while alive, after having been wounded with a side arm, as was the case of the nun in Nyanza.

It's very hard for me to find the appropriate words for such atrocities. I will simply say that this was the fulfillment of a devilish plot, devised by people who were greedy for power and wealth, who chose to be degraded to a lower rank than animals. However, I must also say that there are people who have even risked their own lives during these days to bring some children to the orphanage.

There are also several simple and kind-hearted persons who know the true meaning of love. These people represent the future. Thanks to their sufferings, their praying, and their true Christian charity, will be the ones to draw the Divine mercy on their people.

Nyanza, 9 May

This morning I called Gikongoro, and I have been informed that almost all of the students at the

Marie Merci Institute in Kibeho were killed last Saturday. They were 90 teen-agers, all of them younger than 17 years of age. Only four of them survived, though seriously wounded.

Yesterday, Sunday 8 May, four young girls trying to join their families were killed not far from us. Everyday they kill scot-free. Not even infants are being spared: they say they are "snakes". We are afraid that they will want to pour their rage onto the orphanage where so many children have found protection. We are waiting for someone to come and help us, to comfort us, to protect all of us.

We are in a precarious situation, supplies are running short, and we haven't received any help so far.

How many times have we been dreaming of leaving, of deserting, of crossing the border!

But we all know very well that, should we ever leave these children, it would only take a few hours for the tragedy to be committed. Anybody having Tutsi features would be put to death. The others would starve to death as the orphanage would be sacked.

At any rate, after listening to the radio broadcasting last night, we doubt we would even be able to cross the border at this stage.

They have announced that the enemies will attack from Burundi. As the border is only 15 kms away from here, it means that in case of an attack we would be caught between exactly two fires. What a dreary outlook! Still, a less tragic position, if compared to Kigali: there, we would be caught between four fires.

The Patriotic Front is determined to win the war, and bring down this government of "murderers", which they refuse to recognize or to negotiate with. Only the armed forces still have to declare their opinion. We'll see how this will end up.

Nyanza, 11 May

Father Eros has been sick for already three days now, and more children are coming in. This morning we ran out of water but we were lucky as water pipes in a nearby house, which is now empty, are sound, and we could get some supply.

Until now, we got away with enough food and room arrangements to put all the children up.

Yesterday, the sub-prefect provided us with some passes, which we think of using when Father Eros will recover.

It's 1.00 p.m. Father Eros has a strong attack of malaria. We fear the worst. He can't swallow any more, and he vomits the Fansidal soon after taking it. We have been looking for some Kinimax, which we don't have right here, and, eventually, we found it at the hospital pharmacy.

It's 2.30 p.m. The attack slows down. A Red-Cross car comes along with a military escort. They suggest taking Father Eros to hospital in Kabgayi. He leaves very soon with the European personnel who has come for him.

It's 3.00 p.m. The prefect in Butare comes and visit us. It's a short visit, although very positive for our security. He, together with his staff is desperately looking for some international help; I insist we must protect the children.

I try to help him understand that children can draw some international attention. He answers that all children, regardless of their race, must be welcomed. I can't but think that he is a very poor preacher!

The children we have given shelter to so far are more than one hundred and fifty, most of them being Tutsi.

It's 4.00 p.m. I am informed that the four-month old baby-boy, whom we baptized yesterday, has died. We will bury him tomorrow morning. His granny had taken him to the orphanage after days of dread, and stayed over to take care of the only survivor of her family!

I had a talk with the Rwanda brothers (two seminarists from the Rogationist Brothers) about what the next steps to be taken. I hope that they will not continue to hide away but will start helping for the wellbeing of our community instead. They have understood and picked up courage, and will positively get down to work.

It's 10.30 p.m. I take an inspection tour to check whether all the young people are at their posts. They tell me that they are preparing a few drums to collect the water as it's starting to rain.

A 4 year old boy is moaning. One can't but feel sorry for him, his lips are split, and he can't eat. I gave him some candies and had some sweetened water prepared for him, which he drinks from time to time. He is shocked. I think he was hit several times on his belly.

It's very painful to see children die right before your own eyes, especially this child who arrived here after three weeks of privations and with his look filled up with terror.

There is nothing we can do for him, we are waiting for a doctor to come and save at least those who can be saved. The number of sick people is increasing, the organizational problems are multiplying, while the available rooms are overcrowded and children are sleeping one against the other over a few mats. The infants need milk, but we don't have any. We live in confidence, although we often happen to cry, but we soon recover our hope and start to comfort the others.

Very close to our house there is a roadblock from where you can hear somebody laughing in the middle of a racket; every day they kill someone. The radio keeps saying that the atmosphere is calm again, that one can circulate freely. They have been lying for more than thirty days now. Who knows whether we will be able to cope with the situation and if the international agencies will manage to come over soon, to instil new courage in these young innocents!

Nyanza, 12 May

I'm reflecting on the baby I baptized and who

died yesterday. I had named him Jean-Baptiste, his brother Alexandre being his godfather. The ceremony was touching, simple, and discreet. His funerals, too, will be simple, with two girls in white, three bunches of flowers and, most important, our praying and the attendance of all the children.

I couldn't preside over the mass. At 7.30 a.m., I heard someone screaming at the entrance door. I ran downstairs, and I saw several people from outside who had succeeded in passing our fence and who were beating a woman. I shout at them for having entered the orphanage without any permission, and tell them they are thieves, and that if they don't respect the others, they will never be in a position to claim any international support.

They run away leaving the woman, while a mob starts to form. I shout again, that only authorized soldiers are allowed to enter the orphanage, while no one else can. The situation becomes critical, and all the young boys from the orphanage gather around me, ready to attack. These people are afraid: their chief comes forward and tells me that "they need this woman". I reply that the woman will stay at the orphanage, and that they should never dare again pass our fence; otherwise our guardians will treat them as if they werethieves.

I phone the sub-prefect to explain the situation, and then I also call the prefect. Some minutes later, the gendarmery captain calls me back and says that they will come as soon as they can.

The captain comes with five gendarmes and we talk

about the incident. Upon his request, I give him the list of people at the orphanage, and I show him the forms of those who came in last. I have a feeling that they are specifically looking for somebody's children. They ask me whether we want some military support during the day. I thank him, and explain that we already have a worker, a former soldier, who grants us his protection. Would he be so kind as to give him a weapon instead?

After questioning Albert and having checked his documents, the captain agrees upon my request. We have to be at the gendarmery to collect the weapon at 2.00 p.m.

While leaving, they take the car a trader had given us.

The workmen tell me that, while I was speaking with the captain, the other gendarmes delivered the woman to those standing outside. She was put to death with a hammer stroke on her head, and then thrown into the ditch filled up with corpses. Only a few meters are left to complete the filling of that ditch, which is 25 meters deep and 2 meters wide.

On our way to the gendarmery, I see people standing at different roadblocks; they look afraid. One would say that they have received severe warnings, meaning some threats, should they ever start again. The achievement of cooperation is at stake, especially now when they have exhausted all their subjects as well as their strengths, and for some reason nobody is helping them. On our way back, they become even more afraid when they see we are carrying a weapon; I speak to them, and give them a talking-to. I can tell they feel ashamed.

At our doorway, our guardians inform me that children are not being touched any more at the road-blocks. They left them go, and even direct them to the orphanage. I assume that the prefect has under-stood the message I sent to him when he came here: "Children may touch the international community and it's through them that we must look for help".

He had been considering this for a while before agreeing with me. Today, more than sixty children have arrived. Our dorms are overcrowded. We stri-ve to find some place for everybody in any way. We are turning into a refugee camp, and I expect that we will be organizing two working shifts very soon.

Tonight, another child died. He was 11 years old. He had arrived in a pitiful state and, probably, he suffered from asthma. Our only consolation is that our children have a Christian burial, at least them. This child couldn't recover from the strokes he had received on his head and in his stomach.

All his relatives had been killed. He is also lea-ving for heaven after some hours in the throes of death, and being accompanied by the praying of his fellows and by the love of the mothers living here, and who, have lost their children themselves.

Among the new arrivals, we have a nine year old girl from Mubuga who walked for over 120 kms, carrying her little sister, who is only a few months old, on her shoulders.

We were happy to see them arrive although we cannot restrain our tears, whenever faced with these cases. She had been wandering about, did not know where to go, and is left with a no family member. I do not know who told her of the orphanage.

Some of the children are sick. We badly need a doctor, and we are still waiting for someone to come and give us some help. We are not running short of confidence and goodwill, although our strengths are weakening.

I hope that Father Eros is getting better. Tomorrow, I will be paying him a visit as I will have a military escort.

Nyanza, 13 May

I went to Kabgayi, being military escorted. Father Eros has recovered, but he still needs a lot of relaxation to regain his strength back in full. The community of nuns that has welcomed him made an excellent impression on me. I updated him about the situation at the orphanage, the difficulties on the roads, the roadblocks, which have increased and the disreputable people controlling them. I was accompanied by a soldier who was supposed to protect me.

Nyanza and Ruhango are on the alert. Many people are coming from Bugesera*.

The military camp in Gako is in the hands of the Patriotic Front.

---

* *Rwanda south-eastern region.*

While driving, the soldier tells me that the enemy keeps bombing, while they haven't got any bomb.

I stop in Gitarama to meet the Italians at Astaldis*. The entire population seems to be at a loose end, as the city has been invaded by people coming from all over the Country. Close to hospital, I can see many sick people and wounded soldiers. How difficult it must be to live in such a city!

Nyanza, 15 May

It's Sunday, and another week has gone by! We never missed God's protection, and the water supply problem is temporarily solved.

About noon, two doctors of the Red Cross arrive from Gitarama and inform me about Father Eros. They are the ones who are taking care of him. They tell me that he needs to recover his strengths, and that they will allow him to leave the hospital towards the week end.

I give them a letter asking for blankets, mattresses and food, and addressed to the Catholic Relief Service. Tomorrow, they will come and pick me up to go to Butare together.

It's 8.30 p.m. Maria Mukakalisa, one of the little girls escaped from Kigali, has passed away serenely in Emma's arms. She had been sick for three days; she was of a very delicate constitution, and couldn't endure a malaria attack. She will add up to

---

* *Italian company engaged in paving the Gitarama-Kibuye route.*

the angels praying for us up in heaven, praying for the peace to come back in Rwanda. May her suffering originate the fruits of a true Christian love. She was only six years old.

Nyanza, 17 May

It's a rainy day. We are still looking forward to either some change or a visit. Every day that goes by, we thank God for being our Providence and giving us life. When remembering the dreadful days we have been through, we burst out crying. That memory makes us sick and shudder out of horror. We will never be able to forget all that we have seen with our own eyes, all that we have endured through for this month and a half.

In this orphanage, where we have found shelter and food, we have experienced really tragic moments. The opening of hostilities started here, in Nyanza. Every single day we could hear shooting, people being captured and taken away to be slaughtered, women and children, adults and old people, anybody trying to flee would become the preferred target-shooting for soldiers. These people were not used to hearing shooting, so they couldn't understand why they were being hunted down nor what fault they had. Mothers trying to protect their children were cruelly maimed and massacred with machete strokes.

Most of them were condemned for no other

reason than that they belonged to the Tutsi race.

The first days were just atrocious. People were looking for refuge in the orphanage, and we had to persuade them to go to out in the open country, as this would have been their only way out. We knew that soldiers would have come in and even killed the children, as they did in Kibeho, in the church where thousands of people of all ages were massacred with some grenade shots first, and then finished with hatchet strokes. A large common grave for them, then the fire that destroyed the entire parish.

This sort of thing wasnít only carried out in Kibeho. Between Butare and Gikongoro alone, similar crimes have been repeated in more than fifteen parishes; in some parishes such as in the Kaduha one, more than ten thousand people have been killed.

Today, a large number of parishes does no longer exist; all the work realised through so many sacrifices has been wiped away. In these parishes, over one hundred thousand people have lost their lives.

Our community is growing very fast and has been faced with some logistic problems since the beginning of May.

Children flock in small groups. Each one is in a state of shock, with a long story to tell. Many of them are wounded in their heads, arms or legs. Wounds have all been caused by some kind of knife.

This is the week of horrors. Searches go on. Human madness is now unlimited. We are not surrounded by humans any more but by bloodthirsty savages. They speak of pregnant women being ripped open, of old people whose legs are smashed before being finished of, of young girls being maimed, of men cut up to pieces.

No town in Rwanda has been spared. On the radio, they speak about two hundred thousand people dead, but I actually think that this figure is much lower than reality. Considering the news I have been collecting, the number of people who died is much higher than one million and a half, Some day, history will tell us.

This is not only a genocide, this is also an ecocide. We can observe the destruction of wide woody regions with the purpose of forcing people out of their hiding places.

Man has lost his wits lowering himself to the rank of a beast, without any more feeling and with an appalling fierceness. There are people who are killing those with whom they were living in perfect harmony till the night before.

The tragedy which is going on, will brand mankind for ever. We are going through terrible moments, the reason of which escapes us. No place is safe, the country is laid waste by the shooting and bloodshed. Everybody does whatever he/she feels like doing. The authorities incite the crowds to get armed and destroy the enemy.

We wonder who the enemy is, if all institutions have been ousted by a devastating fury.

Teachers had their throats cut, doctors were

punished with death, traders were first robbed and then killed, and those who belonged to a different party were cruelly murdered.

They killed Tutsi first, then those who were married to a Tutsi woman, then those belonging to another party, and, eventually, prefects and mayors who opposed the slaughtering. This is the case of the mayor of Nyanza, of the prefect of Butare and of some other military officers.

The Presidential Guard and the Troops are not at the front. They have stayed on to slaughter the innocent civilians and state that "no Tutsi people will remain in the country, and future generations will not hear about this race". They murder infants as well, under the pretext that they are "snakes".

The Church has paid a heavy toll.

Only five priests are left in the Gikongoro diocese, two of which are European. The last three priests who were arrested, were first putting jail in Butare where the prisoners refused to kill them. Afterwards, they were taken back to the Gigonkoro prison where they were savagely massacred. For these priests, Father Ireneo Nyamwasa, Father Canisio Mulinzi, and Father Aloyisi Musoni, and for those who were arrested at the orphanage, i.e., Father Callixte Witonze, the priest of the Nyanza parish, Father Jean Bosco Yirirwahandi and for Father Innocenti Nyangezi, we offer our prayers to God. May their sacrifice obtain the peace we all wish for in their country.

The situation is absolutely tragic in any Rwandan

diocese: entire communities have been wiped away, parishes have become graveyards, schools have become famous for the slaughtering that has taken place inside of them. Even in some hospitals, soldiers have dared to kill the patients, while some refugee camps have been destroyed. Nothing has been spared.

Behind all this, stand the one party of the old regime, the soldiers and the armed militia.

Many people were bullied into this escalation of violence, while others joined in to take personal advantages; on the other hand, many suffer silently, trying to protect other people, to the point of endangering their own lives.

From time to time, someone takes some children to us and says: "Father, we are threatened if we hide anybody".

Soldiers, too, are taking children to us, and this makes us hope and gives us courage. Once they accompanied fourteen of them, all in one group, three young girls among them had been seriously wounded in their heads.

Nyanza, 18-19 May

We are still waiting for the situation to calm down. We have some cases of dysentery at the orphanage, and we had to devise an isolation ward. We have no water problems. The adults do the cleaning regularly. How long will we be able to stand this situation? The menace is increasingly pressing around us. At last, the journalists arrive together with Father Eros, which is a great joy for us! I was asleep when they arrived, and have been greatly encouraged! Some Europeans at last! News, letters from my family, and I can't keep my tears back...

The journalists announce that they are coming to stand in for us, and that we must go back to Italy. We have actually got used to all this, and leaving our children is not going to be easy. We hope we will be able to take all of them to a safer place as soon as we can. We share the little food we have left around the dinner table. This is an all together different dinner. And, at night, while sitting outdoors, everybody tells a little bit of his own story of these last terrible months. We spend the night sleeping more peacefully. The arrival of journalists has opened people's eyes to the fact that the orphanage is not isolated; the Whites are a guarantee. It's already late at night when I can read my letters from home, after shutting myself up in my room to hide my tears streaming down my face. We are facing some problems with our personnel. Some of them, besides their specific physical illness, feel the grief of having seen their beloved been murdered. It's difficult to accept such a reality. They are left all alone, and we, we are their only family.

Nyanza, 20 May

Friday morning, 20 May, I take the journalists to

the Burundi border, with a military escort. The situation is difficult. They let me pass without too many formalities, since they know who I am. I hear them saying "It's the Father of the orphanage", but I perceive that their smile has been put on. In return, they require our escort to show his documents; it's somewhat funny, absolute chaos is ruling down here. From time to time, I offer a cigarette to appease the tension of those who seem willing to create some difficulties, or I might address them with some courtesy title so to make them feel important. It's then that the fearful man reveals his real self: he greets me, he asks how I am doing, he smiles at me. Very little effort would have been enough to avoid this war; taking a stand on the very first day would have settled the issue with a few victims. But we thought that it was a showdown "between Africans", and we have abandoned them to their own destiny.

At the border, I meet the Italian Consul, Father Giorgio, Doctor Mussi, Alexis Briquet, Renata Pisu, Luciano Scalettari, Nino Leto, a press photographer for the Italian magazine "Famiglia Cristiana", Fausto Biloslavo, a journalist. We say good bye to Gian Micalessi, Federico Marchini, and Claudio Monici, a journalist from the newspaper "Avvenire" (some of his articles are published later on in this book, editor's note) who are leaving for Burundi. We are not alone any more, there is a future waiting for our children. The bishop, Monsignor Jean-Baptiste Gahamanyi is alive! We are going to visit him in Butare.

He is staying with some of the priests who have

survived the massacre. I am happy to meet him again. He is a man who has been suffering a lot, he tells us that the Rwandan people need help, he asks us not to forsake them, since we are all necessary. Many innocents are still suffering unfairly. This is an invitation as well as a request that goes directly to our hearts. Joy may break out in Nyanza at last! A new chapter is starting for both the orphanage and us.

We have lived through the most tragic moments of our entire existence together with these children. We have been suffering together, and we will continue to work for them, to help them rebuild their country in concord and in peace.

Nyanza, 21 May

We pass on the instructions, we update the newcomers on the situation, we introduce them to the staff. The burden of the activities is now being entrusted to them, together with the smooth running of everything.

Emma is encouraging the others as is her habit. She still has a strong faith, she prays and hopes for her people and for the children who have already started calling her "mamai".

My thoughts go to those priests, nuns and believers who were killed; I think of the many people who risked their own lives to save a few neighbours of theirs; I think of the children telling us they had found shelter with some helpful people as well as of the soldiers who brought children to be hidden by us. Simple people risking their own lives to save their neighbours.

It's 3.30 p.m. as we leave the orphanage. In Butare there is an infinitely sad atmosphere. Not to far from the border, the last roadblock put our patience through a severe test. Eventually, they let us go, by the time it's 6.00 p.m. We are in Burundi now.

Our thoughts and thankfulness go to Doctor Mussi and Father Giorgio Vito who have taken over our task of protecting our children.

I am sure that thanks to their generosity and availability they will serve our children's cause very well.

It's already getting dark. I really have no idea of what I could do in Italy to save my little ones, war is roaming, diseases are at our doorstep as children are now over six hundred in one facility, which was originally designed to shelter one hundred and fifty; the dry season is approaching and water is running out. May God grant us the joy to see our children smiling again.

CORRESPONDENCE SENT
BY FATHER VITO FROM NYANZA

Nyanza, 2 May 1994

My dearest Mom,
my dearest brothers and sisters,
my dear friends,

I hope that you will receive this letter very soon, so that you can have my news and be updated on the events taken place over the last weeks in Rwanda.

I found myself in a very special situation. God has given me enough grace to escape with 62 people who were with me, and who have been spared, thanks to my presence. We all managed to leave Kigali and made it safely. Now we are in Nyanza, in the southern part of the country, where the situation seems to be quite calm: we have not had any problems up to now. We are striving to provide for the needs of our children as well as we can, considering the restricted means we have access to. Don't think I wouldn't appreciate being able to leave. I could have left, while letting everybody else die. As a priest, I did not have the courage to forsake them. I commit my hope to Providence, and I am sure that God will continue to support and protect us.

We must also hope that things will calm down,

and that we will have a chance of leaving. Many people have already returned home some while ago; we stay on to comfort these deserted people.

What shall I say about the thousands of people left with nothing at all? What shall I say about people who don't know where to go and keep wandering around! Only we, who are White, who have now become something rare, succeed in reassuring them a little bit, in giving them a glimps of hope.

I have often thought of you, and I know that you are concerned about me. God will enable me to come out alive from an impossible situation, and I am confident that He will give me all the necessary strengths to see you again. Please pray for peace to come back to this people.

If all this had happened only a few weeks later, I would not have been here with them, but this is the way things went.

At the moment, there are a little more than three hundred of us, considering the newcomers who have just escaped the massacre. I expect more people to arrive, each one having a sad story to tell. Adults are taking charge of general chores, while we take care that nothing is missing. Daily cleaning is ensured, older boys work in the garden, older girls take care of the younger ones, while those mothers who have lost their entire families have again found a reason to live for.

On April 23, two children arrived, one of them, a girl, had been walking for more than 30 Kms.

When I saw her coming in, I was touched. She was leaning on a stick, having one of her feet wounded. She is seven years old and her name is Claudine. I think we are going to be faced with a lot of work to do in the next days to put up all the children who are coming from all over the Country.

Rwanda will never be the same again. Many friends of ours have left, either for heaven or to go back home. Very few Whites have left between Butare and Gikongoro. People are starting to ask for our help. They have not as yet realized that this war, which a handful of fanatics caused to break out, has already destroyed decades of their own history.

Yesterday, May 1st, the Italian Consul came to visit us. We could in the end have some news, and he has announced a possible evacuation. I am entrusting this letter to him.

No Southern towns have been spared. Last week was just terrible. The orphanage has not been involved, though. Better still, every night some soldiers come to stand guard, and protect us from the gangs of thieves.

Now the real Rwanda tragedy is starting: disease, hunger, insecurity, and so on. Until now, we have been lacking nothing. We have not starved nor gone thirsty. Our children, from the youngest to the eldest ones, are all fine.

Two days ago, some soldiers brought in fourteen children and three young girls. Five of them were wounded. We are running short of medicaments, and we hope to receive some very soon. We also need some medicines. Everything is okay in Gitare. People have defended both the parish and the institute.

Father Eros and I support each other. We try to keep our spirits uplifted. We deeply hope that all this tragedy will be over as soon as possible.

Don't worry about us. We are in God's hands. If our sacrifice helped save all these human beings, it means that it was worth going through it all. We are serene and full of hope. Our sacerdotal life has been filled up of its real meaning if we are now left only with what is essential, as all that we ever owned has helped relieve and comfort the suffering surrounding us.

I send you all a loving hug.

Vito

Nyanza, 9 May 1994

Your Right Reverend Excellency**,

Following the fatal events of the last month here, in Rwanda, considering that the situation has not changed during these last days, at least as regards the rough capital punishments of those belonging to the Tutsi ethnic clan, as well as of those trying to escape the massacre; considering

---

* *Vocational training school for young girls aiming at religious life.*
** *This letter was never sent by Father Vito to his Excellency the Papal Nuncio of Burundi.*

that since this week a lot of children are wandering about aimlessly throughout the entire southern part of the country and are savagely put to death with no scruples at all (according to the witnesses of children who have luckily arrived at the orphanage, and confirmed by adults), and considering all the facts mentioned above, I am kindly asking you to obtain an international protection for my 300 children.

We do not want the homicidal fury of somebody to hurt so many innocents ever again.

I trust in your help, and place my trust in Providence, while I remain, Your Right Excellency, very truly yours and while assuring you of my prayers.

Father Vito Misuraca.

Nyanza, 15 May 1994

My dearest Edy*,

A month has already gone by since we arrived here in Nyanza. The orphanage is being protected. Children keep on coming in and continue to tell their atrocious stories, which go well beyond any imagination.

Most of them are really young, younger than 8 years old. Many of them have been walking for over

---

* *Father Vito's cousin.*

50 kms, living on the quiet, fearing to be caught and killed. Here life has lost all meaning: they kill anybody, for no reason at all: adults, old people, children.

We are waiting for the international community to show up and grant at least a minimal security. Today, two doctors from the International Red Cross have arrived, and have visited our children, saying they will provide for a regular service. They are based 30 kms away from here. and are Swiss.

At 8.30 p.m., our beloved Mukakalisa passed away in Emma's arms. She was under a malaria attack for three days, and was also very weak, to the point she could not stand it anymore.

Three children have already died here, at the orphanage. If we had been under normal circumstances, we could have taken care of them. They will pray for us, and I am sure they will obtain our Divine Father's grace thanks to their innocence.

At the moment, we have over 480 children. They keep flocking in, they are all under terrible shock. They tell us that all their relatives have been killed, as they go on crying. I encourage them: from this moment onwards, this will be their home. We still succeed in finding some place for them.

We still have some supplies. We hope that the horizon will open up a little bit in this country and it will be possible for life to start smiling again.

Edward and the other children are fine and say hello.

On my side, I'm looking forward to seeing you soon, meanwhile, I'm sending you a big hug.

Vito

SOME REFLECTIONS
UPON HOPE

Now that I'm back to my notes again, a year and a half after the events taken place, I realize that a lot of things has changed in my life as well as in Rwanda. I am still here with my children, I'm working for them, and still struggling despite the thousands of difficulties to grant them a serene future, to see their faces and their hearts smile again, to see them confident again. All this makes me reflect even more deeply on the Rwandan tragedy, of this country of the thousand hills, but, alas! Today only crammed with thousands of common graves, where thousands of innocent men, women, and children have tragically left their mortal remains.

I am still pondering over the reasons lying behind all these absurdities. I try to understand. I listen to those who try to explain by their abstruse arguments the events, the history, the deep reason of an apocalyptic tragedy where human madness has become common logic and the ethnic cause the motive of so much absurdity.

A tragedy where the most lethal weapon, together with the machetes, was this tiny transistor radio that everybody had, and through which they launched messages inciting people to join the slaughtering project, while alternating them with pious religious songs.

A tiny radio, which had succeeded in corrupting an entire population, causing it to fall prey of a foolish madness, which is unworthy to be considered human. A tiny radio, which would incite people to participate in the horrible misdeeds, while forcing them to exile. At heart, those who made all the plans knew in advance what they actually wanted. It could have been the fear of loosing the many advantages deriving from power that pushed them toward the total loss of their reason being replaced by insanity. And they dragged their own people through the mud with them, degrading their name and dignity.

Those who believed they could solve all problems through murder have forgotten that they will have to give an account for all their crimes to justice, both human and divine. At that point, all guarantees signed by men or by some bureaucratic quibbles will become vain.

Sooner or later, those who are liable for this will have to give an account of their actions. The Rwanda tragedy has been followed live by the worldwide media, which has showed atrocious scenes, of an unprecedented violence as well as foul massacres, but which has very seldom showed the generous actions of those who have made it possible for many people to survive, even when capital punishment was ordered against them fot their heroic stand.

Generosity doesn't create any great sensation. It finds little space among the many different events reported by the news. I have tried to imagine all these young people who, with a rifle in their hands and at their own lives' risk, would take on their shoulders the children found still alive along the way, before resuming their march. These young peopleknew how to be generous despite all adversities. I consider these acts as being more sensational than any other misdeed, because they alone can rehabilitate human dignity.

Ordinary people have proven they could accomplish heroic and disinterested gestures; real, sincere, and deep feelings sprang from their hearts, thus showing the nobility of their souls and the deep faith characterizing them. The solution to many problems, the force to carry out simple and real acts, which will become the basis for a wider dialogue resides in the hearts of those who are capable of making a choice in favour of life - regardless of any adversity or opposite opinion of those surrounding them. A necessary dialogue that will originate from the goodwill of those who never stained their hands with innocent blood. On the contrary, they might still be today's victims of the oppression of those murderers who fear they might be isolated.

Today, Rwanda needs to demonstrate some concrete acts of human solidarity, to commend to the worldwide attention a new image, capable of wiping out the old one. There is a need for concrete acts that, while leaving out any trace of personal grudge or retaliations, would nonetheless manifest the will to assert oneself in is or her full right. There is a need for acts, which may reestablish confidence in the people, as well as instilling hope in the younger ones. There is a need for acts, which may speak about man, as a child of God.

94

It is often the case that when man commits a mistake, he strives to find a reason to justify his own actions to himself and to the others. He believes that these justifications would release him from having to give an account to God, who created him in his own image, for all of his personal responsibilities.

Every man bases his entire life on a set of values he believes in, i.e. values his family and his original society have inculcated in his mind. When it comes to his personal choices, though, he often has to compromise and his decisions are less free. The more compromises he accepts, the less personal freedom he has.

I wonder how many of those who murdered others around them were forced to do it under the threat of capital punishment; how many participated actively, and stained their hands and their hearts, especially, with crimes that they would have never dreamt of. Nonetheless, they had a choice, too. Maybe, today they have become a prey to remorse for having killed beloved people, while they themselves have neither a family nor a home left, they are at somebody else's mercy, with the outlook of being still used as cannon fodder.

I also wonder how many of those who were forced to kill rebelled against the orders, by refusing to commit such atrocious crimes, thus resisting those who wanted to violate their own conscience and break God's law.

Those who survived such a violence have gained

the credibility to solve the problems of their own country.

Dear friend, I am addressing you, who will be reading the pages of this book. The writing style is not sophisticated, but these pages are the outcome of those spontaneous reflections, that originated during some difficult and tragic moments of my life. I am addressing you to say that hope is still alive in this wonderful country of the thousands of evergreen hills. You can contribute to give this country the necessary credibility to be rehabilitated before the world's opinion.

REPORTS FROM HELL

by Claudio Monici
reporter for the Italian AVVENIRE newspaper

Avvenire, 9 April 1994
KIGALI, THE TIME FOR REVENGE

KIGALI. Priest-hunt is open in Kigali, with no distinction as for one's ethnic identity. They kill priests and nuns of either Bantu (Hutu), being the majority, or Batutsi (Tutsi) groups.

In the Rwanda capital city, the situation is slipping out of control and the Tutsi minority ethnic clan is being hunted with no mercy at all. This may accounts for one thousand victims already. There is a real risk that the war between the two clans will start again, only a few months after signing the peace agreement. A new and tragic "ethnic cleansing" with machete blows is being feared. The Tutsi guerrilla movement has taken up arms again and has declared war to Kigali.

In the capital city, twenty-two to twenty-five priests and nuns have been murdered in cold blood with shots and machete blows. Ten others are reported to have been killed in Gisenyi, a northern town. The papal nunciature in Kigali denounced the events in a report by English BBC. The perpetrators of these murders are said to be the Presidential Guard as well as some factions of the Hutu troops opposing the interethnic dialogue, opposing any compromise with the Tutsi. They have announced they intend to carry on their slaughtering scheme from house to house, hunting for civilians and African monks and friars as well as for those who were part of the government, which was virtually decimated after the murder of most of its political leaders and leading institutional authorities, promoting dialogue, according to some information gathered from the Italian section of the Rwanda Patriotic Front.

In the Parliament neighbourhood, the Presidential Guard attacked six hundred rebels of the Front who were in Kigali for negotiations with artillery shots.

According to some information collected via Brussels by AlfaZeta magazine, three priests, one religious and five teachers of a small seminary were killed in Nyundo. "Other information reports about soldiers breaking into a church in San Charles Lwanga de Nyamirambo - a press release from AlfaZeta informs us - and forcing people out, before massacring an unspecified number of people while shooting at them". At the military Center in Masaka (archdiocese of Kigali), some soldiers have "killed some wounded Tutsi laying in their beds in cold blood". At the same time as Radio Rwanda was broadcasting peremptory orders for soldiers to grant security, some military troops were arresting the Consul of Luxembourg to Rwanda, Mister Shamukiga, an activist of an association for the Human Rights Defence. In Kigali, at the Christus Remera Center, many people were killed, including the Jesuitic Fathers Mahane and Gahigi, five Rwandan priests (Gakwaya from the Gikongoro diocese, Boniface Kanyoni from Butare, Jean-Marie Niyitimana and Nzakuburana from the Gikongoro diocese and Juvenal Rutumbu from the Ruhengeri diocese, the vice-headmaster of the Nyakibanda seminary) together with nine nuns from the secular Institute "Vita et Pax", all of whom were from Rwanda. They were all caught during a meeting downtown. Some Spanish nuns and some Belgian Jesuitic priests werespared.

According to some other AlfaZeta information, some districts of the capital city seem to be calm (Muhima), as well as some regions in the country such as Gitarama, Butare, Byumba, and the town of Ruhengeri.

The twenty-four Italian nuns and missionary sisters working in Rwanda are all fine and have not been involved in the massacre of African religious orders. The most shocking anarchy is ruling over Rwanda. There is no more political authority. One may well think that an umpteenth ethnic cleansing is taking place in Rwanda.

Dozens of Rwandan people, who were working for different humanitarian agencies, were "selectively" killed under their foreign colleagues' eyes. Violence doesn't seem to decrease after President Juvenal Habyarimana's death, who was killed on Wednesday night at Kigali airport together with his Burundi counterpart, Cyprien Ntaryamira. Among the victims, ten Belgian soldiers belonging to the U.N. Peacekeepers sent by Brussels were tortured and shot. They were in charge of the escort of the interim Prime Minister, Lady Agathe Uwilingiyimana, who was arrested in the U.N.

offices and put to death in the middle of the street under passers-by's eyes.

In Bujumbara, Burundiís capital city, the situation seems to have quieted down at the moment. The Security Council of the United Nations, being urgently summoned to examine the Rwandan situation, has required both military and paramilitary forces of central African countries to stop all violent acts and to cease hostilities. The declaration, being approved unanimously by the Council members, urges the U.N. Secretary General, Mr. Boutros Ghali, to "take all measures necessary to grant security" in the Country.

Avvenire, 11 May 1994
A WIND OF HATRED BLOWING OVER RWANDA

BUJUMBURA. Thunderclouds filled with rain, and blown by the south-eastern winds, rapidly pass over the Plain of the Elephants. Dark clouds stretch out over a low sky. This great mammal with its ivory tusk doesn't come any more to Lake Tanganyika to wet its long trunk in those waters.

Only the name is left to remember this large eared animal. The original character of Dark Africa's heart has lost that wild aspect that the English explorers, Burton and Speke, would take pride in observing around the mid nineteenth century.

101

"An interethnic war is like a spreading disease" says Boutros Ghali, the U.N. Secretary General. In an interview released to a European newspaper, he adds that: "Ifwe had sent five thousand men to Rwanda (meaning a real tragedy for both men and things, at the back of the hills bordering Tanganyika, editor's note), we could have settled the issue in forty-eight hours. Now, several months of exhausting negotiations will be necessary". No doubt Mister Ghali has missed out one detail, that it will take many and many days more before the slaughtering ends in Rwanda, thus enabling the start of possible future "exhausting negotiations".

In Bujumbura, firearms have been working with silencers for one week now. The Hutu resistance, the "small" ones of the land, ceased last week after a wide roundup by Tutsi troops, the "tall" ones. "Lay down your weapons, this is an ultimatum", soldiers ordered. On the contrary, the Hutu preferred to leave their republic free and go to the hills with their kalashnikovs, while mortar bullets and outbursts of machine-gun fires were pouring out on helpless civilians.

A wind foreboding disturbances and irritability has been blowing over the capital city for some days. People either selling or buying throng the market under the careful look of gendarmes and soldiers. Everything seems to be wrapped up in the African humdrum life, in a timeless pace and in no hurry. But it is the wind blowing from the hills and the internal part of the Country that keeps bringing to Bujumbura stories of murders, destruction, and of two peoples, the Hutu and the Tutsi, which remain inexorably divided, separated by hatred, their weapons, and the violence of tribal rivalry on the same land. The same ancestral story is being repeated in Rwanda, although the roles have been reversed: here, the Hutu are those who, with their machine-gun shots and machete blows, dictate their terms as well as their "relationships" with the Tutsi minority. One simple word is enough to explain the situation of these two countries, which had been united by the German domination first, and then by Belgian one during the last century: it's hatred. The Tutsi state: "God created us first, then he created the Whites, and, last, the Hutu". Superiority is transformed into absolute scorn towards a race they consider to be inferior. As regards the Hutu, they tell the white man: "If you were a black Bantu, you couldn't but hate the Tutsi because of their arrogance and racism". During their search for the Nile springs, Burton and Speke could realize how much rage had been accumulating during centuries of humiliation and arrogance between the giant peasants, claiming to descend from Egyptian dynasties, i.e. the Batutsi, and the Tutsi, on the one hand, and the others, labourers confined to subordinate roles, i.e. the small Hutu with the big nose, on the other.

The ratio of strength and power is about to change in Rwanda and Burundi. Rwanda is disappearing. Life is fading away. Man is vanishing.

Only borders are left while tens of thousands of starving unlucky beings are wandering, full of uncertainties as regards their destiny: a flight, which will end up with their death. At present, the Rwandan soldiers (let's remember that they belong to the Hutu ethnic clan), who are not satisfied with the "job" accomplished by their neighbours who have fallen on Tutsi country with their machete blows, have already announced: "we are coming now to finish the job". This means that anybody giving shelter to a "traitor" will undergo the same destiny.

Meanwhile, yesterday, after the offer of the Peacekeeping Forces by the Organization of African Countries (OUA), the Rwandan Patriotic Front (RPF), composed of Tutsi rebels who are advancing in a tongs-like way, declared that "any foreign presence in Rwanda will be considered as an invasion act".

Rwanda and Burundi, twin countries, are united by their own borders as well as by their two ethnic clans, which are constantly into mourning. Are Kigali and Bujumbara the two capital cities who share a common fate? In Burundi, the United Nations have already ordered the start of "Phase 3", i.e., the repatriation of families, women and children, of diplomatic officers and of all the western government organisms present in the Country: "After all the problems caused by the hasty flight from Kigali - a European doctor tells Avvenire - and especially after the shock children have had to suffer while witnessing scenes of massacres, they preferred to order the evacuation. "Phase 4" means total evacuation". This is why nobody is working in Burundi anymore, either in refugee camps or in those spots where the refugees are confined. Tens of thousands of Burundi Hutu runaways have remained in Rwanda, deserted to their own fate, without any humanitarian support, a link isolated by war; while in Burundi, in Karuzi and in Kirundo, the thousands of Burundi Tutsi, who escaped from the hills are living barricaded. Whenever possible, some volunteers of non governmental humanitarian organisms stayed with them.

Another night is falling over the heart of Africa. In Rwanda, there are people who might save themselves while taking advantage of the darkness to make the last effort toward safety in Tanzania and Zaire. In Burundi, the Tutsi soldiers are preparing for the rounding up: "Hutu rebels are hiding on the hills and we are going to dislodge them".

But where are they exactly? On which hills? Nobody knows for sure. This is what happened the other night, just outside Bujumbura, not faraway from the monument to the "Unity of the Country" (what a bitter allegory!). There had been a leak of information.

The operation was carried out in Kiriri. Three thousand terrorized people and, when everything was over, about fifty corpses were left behind, according to some French sources. It might be a slightly exaggerated figure after having been on the lips of many. But you can actually observe on one side of the hill the remains of the fires, while the houses are marked by the machine-gun shots. Another night is falling, introduce by the shrills of cicadas and the croaks of frogs. And if one ever asks the soldiers if anything happened in Kiriri, they will answer: "We made a mistake (shooting, editor's note). Nothing happened overthere."

Avvenire, 12 May 1994
RWANDA, THE KINGDOM OF DEATH

BUJUMBURA. Monsignor Jean-Baptiste Gahamanyi is reported to have been seen alive some days ago. He is the Bishop of Butare, the second largest town in Rwanda. He was reported to have disappeared at the end of April, following the violent ethnic cleansing carried out with machete blows. He is of Tutsi origin. An Italian Franciscan missionary saw him last Monday on the church courtyard: they shook hands with tears in their eyes.

Since then, two days have elapsed and violent acts continue in Rwanda, thus making it impossible to know what really happened to Monsignor Jean-Baptiste. Every night, a prayer in his favour is lifted up in Bujumbura, from the chapel of the missionary center where priests and religious orders who were forced to leave Rwanda have taken shelter.

It's a mourning prayer for the two hundred thousand victims of the Hutu ethnic clan's tribal violence, which is pitiless against the Tutsi ethnic clan. A prayer for all the nuns, friars, and monks, the men, the women from Rwanda as well as for some Westerners who were slaughtered.

The person we interviewed asked us not to mention his name in order to "be able to go back to Rwanda and meet my beloved again. At least, those who survived". We will call this person "Father Hope", a name for a peaceful future in a languishing country, a dummy name to avoid any possible problem to this missionary who came back from Rwanda yesterday, after a most hazardous travel to "go and see what has been left of his community". Father Hope is that friar who had met Monsignor Jean-Baptiste and shaken hands with him.

Entering the country is still difficult and risky. Only Fathers and a few western diplomats, duly provided with a safe-conduct, succeed in obtaining to passage, but only as far as Butare. Farther than that "it's the devil there who controls life and death", as the missionary says.

"I left Kigali the day before the outburst of slaughtering, on April 6, and I could not go back till now - Father Hope tells us. I arrived in my area, which is not too far from Butare to see my seven brothers from Rwanda. There, I was informed that one of them had been killed because of his Tutsi origin, despite some soldiers and three white Fathers had been protecting him. But they couldn't do anything about it, enraged people tore him from their hands, and then ...". His voice stops to let his hand continue the story while "drawing" a horrible gesture on his stomach and his throat. His name was Father George.

"After one month of war, I found a regime of terror over there. Soldiers force people to take part in the massacres, thus initiating a wild process - Father Hope adds. - Our house was right on the hill, full of life, people, children. There are no children there any more; you cannot hear the sound of life any more, and the meadows are under an awful silence. All of them are of the same size: "small" (Hutu). There, beyond the hills of Burundi, what is reigning is death. But what made me suffer most, was my feeling of powerlessness against this situation, which cannot be compared to anything else. My brothers told me that some people asked for help as they could not do anything themselves. If they had taken care of any wounded person, that same person would have been put to death immediately. If they had given something to drink to a young girl, she would have been immediately massacred as well.

"There is a general responsibility for all this. Everybody has become a murderer. Those who denounced their neighbour, those who did not protect their working mates. Considering what is going on in Rwanda, I feel discouraged. It is as if decades of evangelization have been of no use at all. But a ray of hope is left in me - Father Hope adds - as when I presided over the mass, many people were crying and suffering for all that was happening".

General responsibility is on the part of those

who chose to be onlookers and merely witnesses to the massacre. These make up the so-called civilized world. A world that would neither lift a finger to defend the slaughtered victims nor say a word in favour of those who are suffering. Where is charity? Where is brotherhood? In Father Hope's opinion, they will have to start all over again in Rwanda, "to be a kind-hearted person doesn't mean anything anymore. Only the ethnic clan is important, and may guarantee life. However, one has to belong to the right clan. If you don't have the right identity card, you are a dead man (in Rwanda, identity documents report one's ethnic origin, editor's note). Nonetheless, should anybody succeed in bribing someone in order to obtain false documents, his/her features would sooner or later betray his/her origin, and should some policeman or soldier or anybody else of the civil militia not be convinced of the document's validity at the check points, or if he is not sure of the ethnic identity, then the identity card would be torn, and death would be certain for this man or woman. The Hutu on the roadblock will take over the task with a few machete blows".

Father Hope shuts his eyes for a while, before continuing his story: "This logic will end up in an extermination as I was informed that soldiers will support the civil militia. Priests are being threatened, some of them have already been killed, even right at the altars inside the churches. Now they will carry on a total extermination.

Then, blood will draw blood once again. They

will kill each other even among Hutu, as we must remember that many families are mixed. Once, women were spared, while now even widows are being killed, and I understand that some Hutu fathers had to witness their children killing, because their mother was of Tutsi origin.

Do you want to know how to stop all this? Well, we must carry on a strong international pressure to stop all weapons entering the country to support the two parties, be it the Kigali troops or the rebels from the Rwanda Patriotic Front. Why is nobody doing anything in this direction?

Because Burundi is a poor country without any natural resource to be exploited. Alas, if only they had some oil! But this has always been the case. The weaker and oppressed people are those who invariably suffer. And it would also be wise for governments to stop sending their help without verifying which way it is going first. Everybody must know that whatever is said to be allotted to the refugee camps is heaped up in the barracks for the benefit of soldiers, generals, ministers. If nobody intervenes, the war will last for a long time."

Avvenire, 14 May 1994
RWANDA, THE SILENCE OF THE HOPELESS

NGOZI. They gather around some fires lit with dry eucalyptus leaves. An acrid smoke fluctuates in the air while the camp is wrapped in a light and persistent haze. Profiles are fluffy, as if in a white cloud. Only four weeks ago, all these people still had their dignity as men, women or children. Now, they stand under the pouring rain, as they wait for some beans mixed with flour to cook in the aluminium pans. Itís the younger children who look after the fire by kindling it with twigs and leaves. They keep still, with their big heads completely shaven. A smile breaks out on their faces as soon as they perceive a musungu (Swahili for white man) is approaching. Some of them run away; others, out of curiosity, follow the stranger very discreetly and with much pride, without plunging their hands into his pockets and without waving them to beg. Silence is not being disturbed by din as there are no children playing in this camp: all you can hear is the rain knocking on the helmets of the Peace-keeping Forces, which the United Nations High Commissioner for Refugees has sent here.

The Mubuga camp, a 12 kilometre track East of the small town of Ngozi, on the Rwandan border, is one of the three largest camps in Northern Burundi. Ten to eleven thousand Tutsi refugees who escaped from massacres in Butare have found shelter here. "How did they make it to here?" We ask the nurses of the international organization "Mèdecins sans Frontiëres": "Walking, and crossing eucalyptus and banana woods". Three kilometres away, there is the Mureke camp with eight thousand people, and toward Bujumbura, in the south, we find the Kiwumu camp with four thousand people".

111

The road, which takes to the Rwanda refugee camps winds up to over 1000 meters of altitude. It could be a fast road as it is paved, but it actually is very slow because of the many roadblocks of both the gendarmery and the Burundi Army, which stop any vehicle: cars, trucks, carts, to control that they do not hide any weapon on board. This is a sign of tension and fear, reflecting the Rwandan war, which also affects this tiny central African country, hostage of ancestral relations between the two ethnic clans, the Tutsi minority controlling the Army, and the Hutu majority without an Army but provided with some armed militia who are already training on the Rutovu National Park hills on the eastside, toward Tanzania.

Young people armed with kalashnikovs and machetes who, according to some witnesses, are being trained by "foreign" instigators, some blacks speaking a mixture of English and Swahili.

The Kiwumu camp, the less crowded one, is at 1900 meters of altitude. At daytime, the sun warms up the air under the plasticized tarpaulins offered by the U.N.: a house with a pressed down earth floor covered with straw. When night falls, the cold takes its revenge and the moisture of the soil pierces into one's bones. Some hundreds of meters away from the camp, flows a rather muddy stream of the same color as clay, which blends in the hill. Its waters are used to do the laundry, to wash oneself, to quench one's thirst.

We meet Alessandra Tramontano, a young blue

eyed lady from Naples. She is wearing a white tee-shirt with the MÈdecins sans FrontiËres logo. At the foot of the Vesuvius, where she comes from, she is a cardiologist specialized in extra corporeal circulation during surgeries for heart transplants. However, in Burundi, she is a "nurse" facing up to whatever need arises. We meet her by chance, while she is distributing a few pils. The only place to chat to her is the white tent of the Day Hospital. A dying man is lying in a corner, on the ground, over a plastic sheet and wrapped up in a blanket (as stretchers are missing). Alessandra, who has already gained some experience in Somalia and Mozambique, says that "this man could be affected by anything. He could even be at the last phase of any illness. All he managed to tell us was that he had escaped from Butare, at night, on foot, and without having anything to eat, he fled for fifty kilometres, as a beaten dog".

The three camps are still temporary facilities. The Mèdecins sans Frontiëres staff is taking care of the problem of toilets and water, while still waiting for the real camp hospitals to arrive. People are obviously under-nourished and dehydrated, lacking the basic sanitary conditions such as organized toilets and drinking water; they are dying around like flies. The international Red Cross and the Red Crescent are operating with Mèdecins sans Frontiëres and the U.N. High Commissioner for Refugees.

"This is not my first time to see refugees. Only a few months ago I was in Somalia, but here, what strikes you most, is their indigence. The survivors have been robbed of everything - Alessandra says - and anybody still having something on him was robbed during the flight. They only are left with what they are wearing. "

The man lying in the corner doesn't make a move. Nothing but an imperceptible start of the arm where the needle of the phleboclysis is inserted. Many cases of malaria have also been registered in the camp. "We don't have only sanitary and alimentary problems here - Alessandra goes on - Young mothers quite often do not know how to use medicines. Either they swallow all the pills together or they forget to take them".

Considering the whole population of the three camps, 17% are children under 5, 27% are under 12 years of age. Many of them are wounded by amputations inflicted with machete strokes. At present, two people die each day. Radio Kigali, broadcasting on behalf of the Rwanda government, reported one million victims two nights ago. A teacher, at the Mubuga camp, said that this figure might raise to two millions, besides as many refugees. From two hundred and fifty to three hundred thousand people are in Tanzania, and are all being collected in one refugee camp, which is the largest in the world.

During our tour around the camps, a Burundi soldier at a roadblock asks us to take a boy with us: he should be around 15 years old. He can't tell his own age but he tells us that his name is Dusengumuremyi, which means "I pray God". He carries a camp-kettle which he doesn't want to open. We must insist to have him speak. He tells us he is looking for his family, but nothing else. He doesn't know which camp to look for them in. Children in the camps have been vaccinated against measles, but a few cases of meningitis have already been registered.

We leave again for Bujumbura. Night travelling is highly discouraged. You might find some blocks on the road crossing the Burundi hills (some huge stones with a log) or even some oil spread on the asphalt, which is even more efficient if it is right at the beginning of a curve. Children in the Mubuga camp come close to the car. They start giggling, and are fascinated by the windscreen. A small plastic bear is hanging from the driving-mirror. It's an animal unknown to them and this is why they are both puzzled and amused.

All of a sudden, they stretch their arms while opening their hands wide. The children are numerous, dirty and ragged.

They are standing on their bare feet in the mud caused by rain. Some tiny hands strive to sneak in through other hands to get as close as they can. None of them says a word or asks for anything.

What a discrete way to beg. We leave the camp, slowly. The engine races, we are driving in first gear to avoid running into some child. The small bear is still hanging from the driving-mirror.

There was a split second when the driver almost betrayed himself. His big hand approached the toy to detach it and give it to the first little hand near the window. But he stopped. He closed the window and we left, never turning back. He knew that what he was going to do would not save any child in the camp, but would only make the rest all the sadder - because they would have considered this plastic teddy bear as a toy to speak to and to help them forget.

Avvenire, 15 May 1994
RUSUMU, ON THE SAFETY BRIDGE

RUSUMU BRIDGE (ON THE TANZANIA-RWANDA BORDER). The troubled and dark waters of the Akagera still discharge, as an uncovered coffin, the gruesome meal, which has been feeding the stream for weeks. Death continues to flow down from Rwanda to strand here and there over the bank or on logs into Tanzania. The Akagera is a river flowing with tears and blood, even if it is no longer encumbered with corpses of men, women, children from Rwanda with their members maimed and their faces disfigured by machetes. These are the victims of the slaughtering carried out five weeks ago beyond this bridge, that has meant safety for many others.

"Corpses were floating by at the rate of 30 per hour - an English delegate from the U.N. High Commissioner for Refugees remembers. We met him on the Rusumu bridge while he was making

an investigation on-the-spot - The river had become the grave for swollen, decomposing bodies, cru-
shing at the feet of these wonderful cascades after a
flight of 90 meters".

Death still flows over the Akangera, even if with
much less virulence: the rate has been decreasing
for the past two weeks. We notice a dark mass of
something that got entangled between the bran-
ches and logs. A back eventually comes afloat, but
we can't say whether it belongs to a man or a
woman.

Here, in Rusumu, at the beginning of the
month of May, three hundred thousand Rwanda
refugees have created the largest refugee camp in
the world in just 24 hours, according to some estimates from the U.N. High Commissioner (five
hundred people, according to Tanzanian sources).

The camp is situated ten kilometres away from the
Rusumu bridge. We drive down the road with Giulio
Ghirini, an Italian entrepreneur born in Eritrea, who
has been living in Bujumbara for 25 years. All along
the paved road, meter after meter, kilometre after kilometre, all one sees is an endless line of people walking.
Some of them are pushing a bike packed with parcels
and different objects. They are trying to reach the
camp before dark. "Look - Giulio says while leaning
out of his Land Rover window - look at the grass, one
would say that a herd of terrorized buffaloes just passed
by ...".

Three hundred thousand refugees passed by
several days ago but the grass never stood up again,

although it came up to one's waist. It was crushed underfoot thousands of people; it was useful to lie down on; it was an emergency shelter. Now it is only anextension of hay. A match would be enough for the wildest fire to break out. There is something that strikes the eye more than anything else: it's the number of children walking all alone, then the women carrying water containers on their heads, mats, foam rubber mattresses, all perfectly balanced. Many children alone, many women alone. "Men either died or are still fighting", as Giulio points out. Right after a turn, we can perceive the camp, at one kilometre as the crow flies, on a hill of the Ngara Tanzanian district. Giulio, who is a land-surveyor, after a quick glance, gives his estimate: "It is about three and a half kilometres long and slightly wider". In this rectangle, the humanitarian agencies such as Mèdecins sans FrontiËres, Oxfam, Red Cross and U.N. are preparing some shelters to welcome the crowds; the blue tents from the U.N. are actually not enough for the enormous human crowd who has been taking the hill by storm.

Rwanda refugees arrived here healthy although exhausted. With the rainy season approaching, they will not be short of sanitary problems "It's like a time bomb - a young Belgian from Mèdecins sans FrontiËres says -, many refugees do not have a shelter yet, and it is most urgent to find a place for them as well".

The number of toilets is not enough and miasmas of urines and feces fill the air. Although cholera is endemic to this region, no cases have been reported so far in the camp of the Ngara district. At the moment, they are concentrated on fighting the attack of dysentery and measles on children.

A little lake spreads out just beneath this town, under the open sky on the hill. This is where three hundred thousand people have quenched their thirst and have been able to wash themselves for the first days. Although they are pumping water to fill some chlorinated tanks, the water reserve will hardly last a month; after that, the lake will be dried up.

Some gigantic bulldozers of the Italian company Cogefar (a road is being built some kilometres away) are banking up the camp "to make room for more tents for sure - Giulio Ghirini explains - but also to avoid that the crushed and dried grass catches fire". The most enterprising refugees have set up a market where one can either sell or buy black beans, potatoes, manioc, umbrellas for protection against the scorching heat of the sun. In Ngara, we are already at more than 1500 meters of altitude. Some other refugees have built a hut, the walls being stakes planted next to each other or two concentric rows of these stakes where the space in between is filled with earth. Furniture is rudimentary: some mats and hides as beds, with a log to rest one's head on, and some bags and iron pots. "Our life has become similar to the dried leaves of these huts" a Rwanda man says, being a former official in Kigali.

Giulio is not a great talker but he wants to point out one thing: "For sure, it is an issue of hatred between ethnic clans - he says - but, let's be careful, hatred may be provoked. Today we cannot agree with anybody bevause these leaders (The Rwandan people, editor's note) are totally wrong. Whether they are "tall" (Tutsi) or "short" (Hutu), those who suffer the consequences are always the weakest ones: the people. These three hundred thousands and all the others have already died in Rwanda".

Avvenire, 17 May 1994
THREE HUNDRED ORPHANS IN RWANDA TO BE RESCUED

BUJUMBURA. Father Eros Borile is recovering. Malaria has altered his blood, but not his obstinate determination to stay in Rwanda whatever the costs. Nothing has brought him to his knees: not the convulsive tremors caused by his body temperature reaching 40 C, not even his vomiting, caused by a stomach, that refused even the little nourishment they could find for him (and not only for him). He is returning today to Nyabisindu (Nyanza), after a full week of blood transfusions and treatments, which he underwent at the camp hospital established by the Red Cross in the small town of Kabgay, at the outskirts of the Rwandan city of Gitarama.

Pier Antonio Costa, former Italian Consul in Rwanda, has come to tell us the good news. Happily, Mr. Costa, now based in Bujumbura (Burundi), was the one who took care of Father Eros and the three other Italian friars who had decided to remain at their mission base in Rwanda. Pier Antonio Costa often returns to Rwanda; he covers the route leading to Butare, and even farther, as far as Nyabisindu where Father Eros, a Rogation friar, and the diocesan priest Vito Misuraca are taking care of three hundred war orphans.

Father Vito's traces were lost soon after the hostilities broke out and the blood of the massacres started flowing. He was in Kigali when the Italian of the Col Moschin troops evacuated his compatriots on April 13. Unfortunately, the Italian soldiers arrived when Father Vito, being forced by the events surrounding him, had already left his house to find shelter for his thirty children with him at that time, as well as for the fifteen Rwandan staff members of the orphanage. During their flight, which took them as far as Nyabisindu, the family grew larger with other children he would collect here and there in the villages or along the road. Children whom the people, and sometimes even Rwandan soldiers, had entrusted the convoy in distress with.

"When I met Father Eros the first time, he was suffering and very pale - Consul Costa is telling us now - but he did not want to leave the orphanage for any reason. Father Vito was really concerned. In

121

the end, when we finally could send a doctor from the Red Cross to the orphanage, and he was diagnosed to have severe malaria, hospitalization became essential. Now, having recovered, Father Eros can go back to his children. He was declared to be missing, but he will even be able to withstand a trip back to Italy soon":

Father Vito Misuraca was left alone to manage the orphanage for one week. He has succeeded in going through this worrying situation, keeping faith to his promise: staying with the orphans. He wrote a letter to his family stating: "The rebels from the Rwanda front are advancing and nobody is spared in the slaughtering. Personally, I could easily leave this country. Immediately, if that is what I want. But who can grant these children will stay alive if nobody remains with them?".

Consul Pier Antonio Costa, while trying to help the two Fathers, these days is also organizing the delivery of food relief and medicines, in cooperation with the international Red Cross and the Catholic Relief Service (CRS). "It all depends upon the evolution of the military situation, he says. However, should we want to transfer the children from Nyabisundu to Italy, I am afraid that the complexity of the operation would go beyond my possibilities, considering the great number of people involved. In order to make it possible for them to leave from here, we would need to reach many agreements with the Rwandan government, as well as special authorizations from all the civil militia controlling the roadblocks all along the roads ".

At present, children's evacuation is the last solution to be taken into consideration, in case the situation should degenerate. According to Costa, eradicating these children out of their extreme poverty, and transferring them over to Italy would be an unquestionable mistake, especially for the psychological impact a completely different world from the one they are used to would have on them. And it would be even much worse to send these children back to misery after having taken care of them and nourished them. The Red Cross working out a plan to establish a refugee camp in Zaire.

Two other Italian missionaries wanted to stay in Rwanda. These are Father Edoardo Garlaschi, a Barnabite, still "active" in Cyangugu, on the Zaire border, and the white Father Giuseppe Lucchetta operating in Ruhengeri, in the North, on the Uganda border. They were both given the possibility of leaving, but neither of them made a move. Two Italians working for the Astaldi Company have also decided to remain in Gitarama: Luciano Raddi and Mattia Irto.

Eventually, an alarm signal comes from Bujumbura. It has been sent by the director of the World Food Program (WFP), the Italian Gemmo Lodegiani, that same man who was sick of "witnessing catastrophes". This does not restrain him, after Somalia, from coming to grips with Rwanda and Burundi refugees, both old and new, thousands of which are present on the gathering sites at the border between the two countries as well as in Zaire.

"We do our best to help over a million people with one third of what we would actually need - Lodegiani says. - We succeed in distributing some beans, oil, salt and wheat, either grains or flour. But our cake is small and I have to cut it into very thin pieces in order to give out at least something to everybody. I am succeeding in maintaining the minimum level of necessary calories to live in the camps: 1,990. I have already warned that if they do not facilitate some of the procedures, especially at the Bujumbura port, and if they do not organize an aerial bridge with Dar es Salaam in Tanzania, where foodstuffs leave for Burundi, in fifteen days we will be facing a real catastrophe, even worse than the one that took place in Somalia!".

Avvenire, 21 May 1994
ORPHANS UNDER MACHETE BLOWS

NYANZA (RWANDA). "It's a rainy day. We are still waiting for someone to come and visit us. Every day, we thank God for giving us life. We have been through dreadful moments ...". Here are two little girls, holding each otherís hand, who have just come to our doorstep. Father Vito Misuraca, in Rwanda since 1978, stops reading the diary he has been writing to keep his spirit busy during these long weeks of madness, although he writes: "remembering make us cry, causing a feeling of horror to arise inside, making us sick of what we

124

have witnessed with our own eyes". The sound of children's voices gathering under the sun comes from outdoors.

And here are two other girls arriving just now. Their names are Denise and Cèline, aged 6 and 7, respectively. Father Vito gives the girls a candy or two and invites them to join the other children in the yard. Denise and Cèline haven't had any news from their parents for three days. They are not sisters, but they ran away together. Some people whom they met on their flight told them that in Nyanza some European priests could give them shelter. Their parents have certainly died, being Tutsi. Should one of them be still alive, he/she would be hunted down in the open country. To stay on the roads is very dangerous for a Tutsi. There are too many roadblocks controlled by Hutu civilians armed with machetes, lances and arrows. There are also some gangs of rascals who escaped the control of the local authorities as well as of the Rwanda Army soldiers. We met them all along our journey to Nyanza and towards the inner part of Rwanda, for about one hundred kilometres.

Before the bloodshed, which turned the country upside down, one hundred and fifty young orphans, ranging from three to twenty years of age, were living at the Rogation Fathers' house in Nyanza. After one month and a half of slaughtering, their number is now over six hundred. Many of them, who were lucky enough to survive, witnessed their parents being massacred like animals. If they are

125

safe, at the moment, it's thanks to a desperate and lonely flight or to the help of some sympathetic good spirit who hid them before entrusting them to the cares of the Fathers at the orphanage now protecting them. Some of them have also arrived here with some soldiers. Two days ago, Father Vito met his brother again, Father Eros Borile. Father Eros, worn out by tension and weakened by a violent malaria attack, had to stay in bed for one week at the Gitarama International Red Cross Hospital, in the Kabgay area, 50 kilometres away from Kigali. Father Vito and Father Eros chose to stay in Rwanda "to defend children" from the devastating madness of Hutu armed gangs stirred up against the Tutsi.

At the hospital, while sitting on his bed, still weak, though recovered from his malaria, Father Eros welcomed us in a semi-dark room: "In Nyanza, the soldiers have protected us by preventing the troops from entering the orphanage. The civilians have quite often tried to enter with their machetes. They were looking for people they wanted to take away." On his bedside table, a book, a History of Jesus, by Arthur Nisin; on one side, a rosary the Father runs through his fingers from time to time. "How many deaths? Many. Too many. At night, you could hear the shooting and the screaming of terrorized people. Now, I understand the situation is more peaceful, but tension remains high". Born 39 years ago in Monselice (Padua) and having been in Rwanda for 7 years, Father Eros has

126

never thought of escaping. Now less than ever would he want to leave the village of children whose eyes reflect the terror of what they have been witnessing to. With some of them, you may easily obtain a smile by offering a small paper plane, while with some others it is just impossible. "We could have left - the Rogation Father says. - The real problem was to desert the children and the staff. Should we have left them alone? Never. To have the children leave the orphanage would have been an impossible venture. It was, and still is, rash to find oneself on the roads without any protection. Our presence, as Europeans on their side, gave them confidence, so we stayed". The same applies to Father Vito, although his story is different. He escaped from the Kigali massacre with three cars where thirty orphans had been packed into, together with some twenty women saved by the orphanage in Remera. A difficult flight lasting three long days. After escaping the fights between the Rwanda Patriotic Front and the Army, his presence was of no use when, at a police roadblock, they took one of his Tutsi helpers out of his hands, the young man was then delivered by some adults to two teen-agers, of about fourteen years of age, armed with truncheons. After having been pushed to the back of a house, this young man disappeared. For ever.

Father Misuraca, 44, from Catania, could finally reach the orphanage in Nyanza. One day, rumors went around that they wanted to attack the chil-

127

dren's village. At that point, the Fathers called the gendarmery for help, who sent two of their men. "Since then, people say that Imana ikinze amaboko (God did not allow the orphanage to be attacked)".

It is terrible to notice how naturally people, but not all of them luckily, have carried out such a massacre. They haven't even spared the children. Lances would pierce through bodies already cut with machete strokes. Women are undressed and maimed. Mothers trying to save their children lost their arms with hatchet strokes. A Rwanda nun was struck on her head with a hammer and then thrown into a ditch, where she died after two days without anybody being able to help her.

Every day new orphans come in; children tell incredible stories of unlimited atrocities. We read in Father Vito's diary: "Claudine is the first one to arrive. She has been walking for 30 kilometres, leaning on a stick the whole way. A machete blow has cut one of her feet open. Her parents have died. Her arrival brought us a lot of joy. We were hoping that others would escape the massacre and have enough strength to reach the orphanage". Many others have indeed arrived since then.

Father Eros is collecting his few belongings to go back to Nyanza: "Many people who took part in the massacres have then taken children to us. We witnessed some acts of genuine goodwill by people who were committing the worst atrocities at the same time, at the very moment in which the tragic acts were been committed. Something really difficult to conceive. It's absurd".

Now the Fathers are asking that somebody or some humanitarian "flag" come to Nyanza to protect these six hundred children. Yesterday, a supporting Rogation Father and an Italian doctor arrived at the orphanage, accompanied by the former Italian Consul in Rwanda, Pier Antonio Costa. Those injured, as this thirteen year old girl with five machete strokes on her head or this other one with a grenade splinter in her skull, will be able to receive the cares of a skilled hand.

Avvenire, 22 May 1994
A GULAG NAMED RWANDA

GITARMA (RWANDA). When we got to the roadblock, he was already under arrest. He is an adult, a man, of about thirty years of age. Or maybe younger. They force him to take his shirt off and lower his pants. This is the dress of a fleeing man, dirty and torn. Civilians with lances and machetes are looking for something. We observe the scene from our car. We also have been stopped for checking despite our safe-conduct issued by the Rwanda embassy in Burundi. But who can read in this corner of the thousand hills of Rwanda? They want to know who we are, where we are going, where we are coming from, and why we have come to Rwanda. They even require the identity card of the soldier with his kalashnikov, the escort the commander of the Gitarama garrison gave us. This is a clear sign that the soldiers feel they are loosing their control over that madness, which has taken possession of people's brains and has stained the hands of the Hutu interhamwe (let's gather, editor's note) with blood. Now these armed civilians are those who are in command, and have power over life and death.

These are the militia armed by Rwanda President Habyarimana, recently killed on April 6, whose purpose was to defend his regime; the former were then stirred up against the Tutsi ethnic clan by the same people who perpetrated the attempt on him. A massacre was intended to prevent the peace agreements recently signed in Arasha in Tanzania from being ratified between the Rwanda Patriotic Front - the Northern rebels, Tutsi children who had taken refuge in Uganda years before - and Kigali. These agreements should have granted equal rights to the Tutsi ethnic minority clan.

This trembling and half-naked man is a Tutsi. And to the Hutu interahamwe, he is nothing but an enemy. He tries to explain something to the one who is keeping a close watch on him while handling a long rusty knife. A jeep with some soldiers has just arrived. For the Tutsi man, this could mean safety. If only these soldiers would take him away from here. But they don't take him and leave instead. He sits back on the ground and tries to recover his shirt, but a militiaman stops him. A group of women together with some old people and children arrive, carrying the youngest ones on their shoulders. Everybody stops. They all put their blankets, mats, baskets down, and show their papers to the "inspectors" at the roadblock - three logs and two stones on the road -: the papers say that the women belong to the Hutu ethnic group. The entire group can continue the journey. Who knows how this man has fallen into this trap? This Tutsi could be put to death at any moment. He will be killed as an animal behind a tree or a wall.

They let us go first. Let them be safe from prying eyes! No witnesses, especially if these are journalists. The Tutsi figure becomes smaller and smaller seen through the car driving-mirror.

In Rwanda, the life of an "enemy" is still not worth a cent. This is inconceivable if we think that when considering some people, which because of their culture and tradition, have - or better, used to have - a deep respect for life, our thoughts turn to the Rwanda people. Many of their folk sayings speak about life. A folk saying in Kinya-Rwanda language goes that one cannot kill a seed: "We win over death by giving life". And it is also true that a "Rwanda person would never trample on a germinating seed of bean". On the contrary, now, down here, life is fading away. They are destroying it by pulling out men, women, old people, children, the "enemies".

It is unquestionably difficult to realize in forty-eight hours what is actually going on in Rwanda, this reign of terror.

But there is enough to see. Enough of disgusting things as horrible as trembling dying human beings or as repulsive as the gulag we went through in Kabgayi where some three thousand Tutsi have been packed in a space as wide as two hectares, where children are sleeping in the mud, where people walk barefoot over excrements and corpses, which have been left there as garbage.

We could enter Rwanda while following a convoy of the International Red Cross: three trucks carrying fourteen tons of corn, four of beans, sugar, rice and olive oil. Rwanda welcomes visitors, on the Burundi border, from a large panel. The Red Cross escort chief waiting for us at the border is accompanied by a Rwanda soldier, unarmed and wearing a white shirt, who has been given the task of interceding on our behalf whenever we meet the roadblocks of the armed civilians. We have counted twenty-eight of them over a distance of some one hundred kilometres. We have also met several threatening interhamwe : an old man wearing a fireman's helmet and holding a lance in his right hand, a young man smoking some grass, who approached us wildly, holding his machete, and who asked the musungu (the Whites, editor's note) whether they were Belgian: a certain passport to death. Another one would exhibit his old rifle, maybe not even loaded, but you never know! In some zones quite remote from the villages, and isolated on this road, these hunting fellows, with their weapons in their hands, are true bandits. But what strikes and worries you most, is noticing boys not older than ten years old armed with truncheons, with extremities as big as a melon: one only stroke would be enough to kill a veal.

The road descending from Gitarama to Butare, some ten kilometres away from here, is covered by hundreds and hundreds of fugitives, all of the same size, meaning "short", though to say that all Hutu are short would be not quite right. Some of them are in fact tall. There are other characteristics that differentiate the two clans, which are at times more subtle than a mere difference in their noses. The Tutsi have a more elegant nose, compared to the Hutu's snubber one.

Those who are running away now are Hutu. The Patriotic Front, armed and supported by Uganda, is strong and advancing. The Hutu fear that they will go through the same destiny they have been reserving for their "enemies" over the last month and a half. Villages are now empty. According to some estimates by the Red Cross in Geneva, from eighty to one hundred thousand people are living in refugee camps. In the villages that we cross, we can count the Tutsi houses, which have been robbed and destroyed after the massacres. Now, the order is to cancel any trace of the massacre, and if corpses have been thrown into common ditches, hoes are now working to abolish the past. Those who had to stand by powerless and witness the genocide explain that nothing must be left of "them", not even a brick. The interahamwe want it this way.

We've been hearing fits of dry coughing all night long. Kabgayi, where we spent the night, is situated at about 1900 meters of altitude. Near the church of the FrÈres de la Croix (Brothers of the Cross), a Canadian congregation, there is a gulag for the Tutsi escaped from the butchery in Kigali. Rwanda soldiers are watching over it. Children, old people, and adults are sleeping right on the ground, in the mud, and the ground is chilly during the night. And this is it. They cover themselves with soaked blankets. Five aligned small heads come out of a blanket. These children are lucky to have found a square meter of grass, however rotten for a bed. Nobody in the camp, either young or old, wear shoes. The stench in the air is nauseating. The sound of axes over timber, which will be used to set the fire, is the background noise of the coughing fits. People contend for a handful of boiled beans. Those who have no dish or cutlery will have to eat directly from the palm of their hands.

A boy and a girl approach us and tell us in English, that in the Kabgayi camp every day a few of them are taken away by armed civilians and killed in the grove on the hill. They speak even if they are well aware that someone could be spying on them. "As an excuse, they accuse the condemned ones of being infiltrated members of the Patriotic Front". This news is confirmed by other sources. Two hours before our arrival on the camp, "at least six people had been taken away, to join those in the ditch". But we can count corpses even inside of the camp. Wrapped up in a red cloth, there is the body of a man, all skin and bones, like a bamboo shoot. And there, in the mud, two motionless and cold feet come out of a blanket.

A third corpse has been laying on a stretcher for some hours already. It was a woman who died during the night. The Kabgayi wretches don't even pay attention to this any more. They pass by, and hope to live a little longer; they do not look at these three corpses - one of them being a twelve year old girl - thrown down, as if they were garbage, in a corner of what, once, used to be the Congregation's dispensary, which now accommodates the sick and the dying. It is in this absolute neglect that men, women, children, old people who cannot stand anymore have to live. They have all been packed together in a place that would be too filthy even for animals.

Avvenire, 24 May 1994
RWANDA, THE U.N. ARE BLOCKED

RWANDA. Does anybody still remember those terrible images shooted by an amateur camera from the window of a building? Do you remember those three men who, from a distance, were roving the streets like jackals armed with machetes and truncheons, and who, from time to time, would violently beat the flesh of this heap of people scattered

135

everywhere over the ground? And the last one who, on his knees, was lifting his hands to defend himself or to implore for his life to be saved. It was a test: the door was opening onto the Rwanda hell. It was entering our homes, and the world. Do you remember how this body fell in the dust after receiving the final stroke, which, finally, put him to death? Remember! It was one of the first films coming from Rwanda, and what we have just remembered took place in Kigali, at the time the musungu, the Whites, were about to be evacuated by international contingents as fast as it could be done. Hardly one month and a half have elapsed since then, six weeks, a time during which a terrifying butchery has taken place in the Country of the Thousand Hills. Something even more murderous than what had happened in Pol Pot's Cambodia, or in former Yugoslavia or in any other sad place of war and death. This one starts by already reporting one hundred thousand deaths, then two hundred thousand, then again five hundred thousand, and now, maybe, one million victims. But you must also recall the heaps of naked and swollen corpses, bearing the marks of torture, who were floating above the Akagera, the river that flows into Tanzania. Those images were a cry for help coming from Rwanda that we have been watching on our TV screens for over a month now. During this time, the U.N. have decided to withdraw their contingent of Peace-keeping Forces, while only leaving an ineffective handful of soldiers there. On May 4, Keith B. Richburg from the Herald Tribune reported from the Rusumu cascades (bordering between Tanzania and Rwanda) and could already assess the figures of the ethnical massacre: "The gruesome procession has been going on for several days; twenty-five to thirty corpses per hour, seven hundred per day, have been flowing down the river". However, as soon as the "flight" of the Whites was accomplished, the information door once again closed down on the Rwandan hell. And here we are, reopening it wide this time to throw the crude news right in the faces of our people, who are taken up by the latest lucky winners of some billionaire lottery, "we announce the international alarm for the forty thousand corpses floating above Victoria lake".

We merely wish to remember that these men, women, and children - with their saponified skin and with some shreds of flesh still attached to their bones - whom are now being shown on TV, well, they are the same corpses who were flowing down the Akagera a month ago, and who, after two hundred kilometres, if crocodiles haven't eaten them yet or if they haven't been stopped by some ravines along the river, have ended up "polluting" the waters of this immense lake. And more of them are on their way, as the slaughtering isn't over. Those whom we do not see are by now skeletons in common ditches. One month and a half has elapsed. Were have we been? Why have we reopened this window only now?

FACING MACHINE-GUNS TO DIE FASTER

BUJUMBURA. The little girl was crying while the man was holding her by the arm. She was imploring: "Please don't kill me, don't kill me", while terrorized tears were streaming down her face. But this man was deaf through both ears and stony hatred filled what used to be his heart. "I was standing at the window, powerless as well as paralysed with horror. The little girl was pulled up by her arms and thrown to the other side. Her shirt got stuck to the meshes of the garden gate. Then I saw that stick hitting her violently over her head. Once, twice, three times, until, because of the repeated counterstrokes, the iron tore the shirt and the little girl stopped screaming, for ever". The person reporting this heartrending execution in Bujumbura is Giancarlo Luzzi, 50 years old, Father Giuseppe Minghetti's right-hand, a secular priest. The events at the end of April in Rwanda forced him to leave the children of the Nyamata orphanage behind 30 kilometres south of Kigali, and to take refuge in Burundi while still waiting to go back to his children. But he is not sure that they are still alive. Now, the Nyamata area is being controlled by the Rwanda Patriotic Front, the Tutsi rebels who, because of their advance, have cut Rwanda into two parts.

The Father and his assistant did not run away. "Get out of here, you, whites, or we will treat you as all the rest" the interahamwe had imposed and promised. These death squadrons belong to the Hutu ethnic clan, and are made up of civilians armed with machetes, lances and some rifles who have been decimating the Country of the Thousand Hills. They have dumped hundreds of tortured and maimed corpses into the rivers, and often these belonged to children, women, men and old people who still had a breath of life in them. A life that was quickly suppressed by being dumped into a common ditch or even by being thrown to the crocodiles populating the Akagera river flowing into Victoria lake, between Uganda and Tanzania, and Rusizi river, a dark colored stream that flows into Tanganyika lake, between Burundi and Zaire.

Mister Luzzi still starts with horror and he covers his eyes with his fingers as if trying to cancel those horrible executions and those cries for help that have been registered in his brains, and which he lives over again in slow motion every moment of the day, as a never-ending horror color movie. He finishes his testimony adding that the young girl, reduced to a dead body in a pool of blood, with a fractured skull, was violated and then beaten again, again with a stick, by the son of the man who had killed her. This boy, a Hutu, was six or seven years old; the young girl, a Tutsi, was 12.

The parishes in Rwanda where the Tutsi believed they would find a respected and feared shelter- as had happened years before when the Country had been shaken on several occasions by other massacres

- have become graveyards, instead; schools and stadiums have become famous for the slaughtering that has taken place in them, hospitals for the patients being killed there and the refugee camps for all the terrorized people running away after being assaulted there.

Father Ireneo Nyamwasa, Father Canisio Mulizi, and Father Aloysi Musoni, three priests of the Gikongoro diocese, were once arrested by the interahamwe and taken to jail. The other prisoners were ordered to kill them, but they refused. This kindness was not repeated at the Gikongoro prison where the three priests had been moved to later on, and where they were cruelly massacred.

And what about the butchery in the Nbazi stadium where people threw themselves against the soldiers' ìwhiteî machine-guns to die as fast as possible, without all that "suffering" inflicted on the flesh by knives and cutting weapons. The following other atrocious story, (but you can count them by the dozen), has been reported to us by another Italian missionary who still manages to enter Rwanda to give some support to his Tutsi brothers living in terror and hiding in some place: "Death reigns over the hill. All the Tutsi from the parish were gathered in the stadium: the most reluctant ones by force. The others, especially the younger ones and the children, out of some trivial pretext. There must have been, at least five thousand people all together. The stadium was then surrounded by the soldiers, but a last circle of civilians armed with sticks and machetes encircled the soldiers from behind. The soldiers started to shoot here and there, and to launch grenades inside the stadium with the aim of forcing the Tutsi to come out and of delivering them to the civilians' rage. But the Tutsi, who had no intention of leaving this stadium in order to be cut to pieces with the civilian large knives, started to throw stones at the soldiers, in order to excite them and provoke their armed reaction. But the soldiers stopped using their weapons all together and started asking for money. At this point, the prisoners piled up all the valuable objects they had and burnt everything: "If this is what you want - they said - you are not going to have anything, and now, go ahead and kill us if you so wish". The massacre was thoroughly accomplished over that night".

APPENDIX
WHAT HAPPENED
AND WHAT IS GOING ON

by Rodolfo Casadei

Two months have already elapsed since the butchery in Rwanda started, but both the press and the international TV still misinterpret a situation which is moving more and more towards a stalemate. The tragedy, which has overwhelmed this tiny African Country, is still being presented as a tribal war, being the outcome of an atavic hatred between twoethnic groups: the Hutu and the Tutsi. But the issue is something completely different. Once and for all, it must be made clear that the Rwanda war (as is the case of other African wars and not only those in the Nineties) is not an ethnic war, but a war where the ethnic element is being exploited in the struggle for power to the advantage of a few limited political Élites and military factions. Being part of a specific ethnic group is not in itself a reality that should give rise to opposing parties, but it does become a contributive factor when competitiveness breaks out, and is then exploited to monopolize the material resources and subsequent power.

This interpretation of a so-called ethnic war, which, actually, can be correctly applied to many of present-day conflicts (Somalia, Liberia, Bosnia, ex-Soviet Caucasus, etc.), applies to the Rwanda situation as well, even if Rwanda, together with Burundi, is the African country where social and ethnic stratification is much more emphasized. In fact, in Rwanda, as in the rest of Africa, the ethnic issue has been completely transformed by the colonial stage, to the extent that we may well state, without exaggerating, that present-day African

144

ethnic groups are the result of both colonialism and post-colonial political experiences.

In pre-colonial Rwanda, relationships between the Tutsi and the Hutu took on a feudal character: the latter would pay the former in kind, who in turn would grant them their protection. The peasant would submit to the warrior just as he would have in Charlemagne and King Arthur's day in Europe. Colonialism has introduced the monetary economy, a western-style bureaucracy, and a modern school system. All this helped standardize the two ethnic groups, both at top levels (those who were studying and becoming rich) and at lower levels (those who could not exploit the new possibilities). But it has also given rise to competition for acquiring new sources of power and prestige within the new class of "modern people": who was ever entitled to modern resources and command positions? And this is when ethnic categories have reappeared, instrumentally: the Tutsi demanded the whole lot of the power in the name of tradition, while the Hutu demanded the same thing in the name of democracy. In 1959, the Hutu were the winners, but only a restricted power group benefitted from the victory until they were replaced by president Habyarimana's group in 1973.

The same issue has been repeated in our days: the Rwanda Patriotic Front recruits especially among the Tutsi, who for sure have not been operating in favour of their ethnic group, which was actually left at the mercy of both government and local gang retaliations, but favoured their political-military leaders instead. The Hutu extremists, who instigated the crowds to slaughter the Tutsi, are also seeking to defend their factious interests and generally not their ethnic ones, as is clearly evinced by the victims of their attacks, after president Habyarimana's death who were the leaders of the opposing parties, all of them being Hutu except one. These extremists covered up the true interests at stake, i.e. the ruthless craving for power, with the ethnic massacre, which had been prepared over a long period, in terms of both propaganda and organization.

The tragedy is that the "base" has assimilated the Èlite's ideology: Hutu peasants and young people, who played a leading part in the slaughtering, have got themselves involved in the tribal war scheme, in order to attain their own material interests. Hutu peasants, because of their steady hunger for lands, have the opportunity of seizing the lands of their Tutsi neighbors who have been killed; young people, who have no credentials in traditional African society, achieve a social standing thanks to one weapon or other placed in their hands, be it a machete or a kalashnikov.

A NEVER ENDING
TRAGEDY

Kigali, 12 November 1996

It is most depressing to look at all these endless lines of refugees wandering about aimlessly towards faraway places they know nothing about, to the mercy of anybody holding a rifle or wearing a uniform, most often creased and in rags, poor people suffering without any hope, looking for food and water, where from time to time only the luckiest or strongest ones among them succeed in finding something to eat. The others, who are less lucky and weaker, just lie down along the street while waiting for some merciful hand to help them raise a little bit, give them a sip of water that might revive them and help them keep hoping and dreaming their land, the tiny house they had to escape from because of the war, the fields, which were supposed to yield a harvest, their beloved ones, some of which are already dead because of privations, while others cut down by diseases and some others are still scattered who knows where. Despite all this grief, they go on hoping to return and find their little things beloved so much, which they had fought for, and had sacrificed so much to save the money necessary to buy them, a drop-by-drop saving, the result of small bargainings in the market of their own village, where everybody would go with their own goods, once a week, and from where they would return home being tired although pleased for the small earnings they had made, but most of all happy, for having met their friends, their relatives, their beloved ones by whom they had been entertained, to be updated about each other and to cheer up with a little beer: "amarwa or urwagwa". A different day, the market day, so different to make one forget the daily routine and toil.

A day one remembers with some nostalgia feelings of regret as even then, at the very daybreak, paths and streets were enlivened with people walking with a cheerful heart and being certain of their destination. An increasing chatter accompanied by birds chirping would wake up those who were still asleep. A merry atmosphere was reigning then, and from time to time, along the path, quite differently to what you see today, you would notice mothers sitting along the street breastfeeding their babies.

All it is today is an aimless, silent and sad walk of thousands of people their faces being disfigured by exhaustion and hunger, with children who cannot cry anymore because they have ran out of tears, distressed mothers who cannot breastfeed their babies, desperate men who lost everything they had and who are unable to protect themselves or their families, carrying a few things on their heads or their shoulders, while looking for a place to rest and to find something to eat, if possible.

This is the tragedy of the countries of the big lakes in the heart of Africa, a tragedy which has upset the whole of mankind as everybody has seen blood-curdling photographs or pictures.

For two years and a half, millions of people have survived in refugee camps, set up as best as they could by the various humanitarian agencies. These camps were planned to be a temporary solution, while finding the final one for all those whom the war had forced to flee away from their land. They turned out to be forced jails, ran by people with no scruples at all, who imposed the rule of the strongest. There was no willingness to find the correct solution for the refugees to the extent that their presence in foreign territories helped give a different image of the host country at first. Then it helped originate tensions and skirmishes on the border line, which were of some use to those who were just looking for a pretext to solve any latent tension. New horizons and new frontiers are necessary in an Africa, which may be willing to find back some peace, but brave men are also essential, who will love their people and will not sacrifice them for unlawful profits deriving from questionable trading. The Kivu war in Zaire is one of the many accounts to render against a government which did nothing but take. Now the day of reckoning is coming and everybody is taking advantage of the vacant power that has been created and of the unfair borders, which had separated entire populations in remote November 1884 and February 1885 in Berlin. One can once again hear the deadly noise of weapons, spreading death and terror, and pushing endless lines of people in the streets, who are fleeing away aimlessly and leaving hundreds of thousands of corpses all along their way, who will probably never be buried. The humanitarian help lavished for all this period and the willingness not to do justice against those who were at the origin of this huge tragedy, turned out to be inadequate, as it was restricted to food alone, which had become a source of large profits for many.

At the Goma Border, 15 November 1996

The last outpost of refugee camps in Zaire has fallen. Corpses in Mugungwa may be counted by the hundreds, people have fled, not to unknown destinations this time, but towards Rwanda, their own country, their home. Neverending lines of upset people whose faces turned ugly because of distress, are going back with everything they can possibly carry. It is difficult to count them: there's a line longer than eight kilometers all along the main road going to Rwanda. Many of them can't make it, and stop under a downpour, just a little faraway from the edge of the street not to be overwhelmed by this human tide, which sweeps away everything while passing by. They are worn out by fatigue, but they never give up the thought of resuming their journey as soon as they can, so as not to be the last ones to arrive in their homeland: Rwanda!

Many of them will have to answer to justice, some others will go back to their daily routine, all of them will remember with sorrow those terrible days of exile, and they will cry for their beloved ones, who died in a foreign land. For sure, their life will be different in Rwanda, and no matter how things will go, it is their own land, nonetheless.

Everybody wonders what will happen to these refugees once they are back in Rwanda: where will they go? Will they ever find back those fields they used to cultivate before the great flight? These questions demand a real and wise answer to avoid the rise of the same presuppositions at the basis of new social conflicts, which would be detrimental to Rwanda society. As at the end of any war, both winners and losers resume their daily lives close to one another, although playing different roles, and society mixes up again being faced with new social requirements on its way to the future. Just thinking of solving problems with new wars and slaughters would mean outlining a precarious future for one's children.

Gisenyi, 16 November 1996

Nobody would have expected such a huge flow of refugees. At every hour more than twelve thousand people coming from Zaire are crossing the Rwanda border. A crowd exhausted but determined to reenter its own country, sick of living in refugee camps, with the steady fear of being attacked and more often without any food for entire weeks. In

152

Rwanda they will find something to eat at least. From the side of international cooperations and for many of the so called humanitarian organisms, it is a flop. Despite all the help their governments gave them, they say they did not expect so may people. Thousands of hands stretch out: it is the fight for survival. The few trucks carrying supplies fear being assaulted by people who had been starving for weeks. The throng is so intense that many people fall being tramples over by others. Brawls arise for a package of cookies, where only the strongest one will be the winner. Trucks then start off again while throwing in the middle of the crowd all of what they have been carrying to prevent it from being assaulted. We are told that the people on their way are still many the other side of the border. They are the weakest ones, the sick, the elderly and the children. Many of them are blocked on the roads and they have few chances of reaching their destination, at least as far as some merciful hands will pick them up and take them home.

One feels especially sorry for children. Many of them cannot find their parents any more; they cry dejected and run without knowing where to go. When they are tired and exhausted, they sit and cry until they can do it, then they lie down and fall asleep along the route and under the rain which is pouring down in this period. A new story is likely to begin for many of them in Rwanda, the country where they were born, but without their parents, who died of either privations or some disease during these two years of forced exile. All our attention is taken by the sad look of these children who don't even dare to ask for something to eat any more, although you understand how hungry they are. They are so many that there is not enough to go around for everybody. So, with tears in our eyes we help the first ones who come. The others will have to receive something next time.

We leave again with our hearts filled with sadness, and we wonder why this country has to suffer so much. At home, in our countries, we are so saturated with wealth that a lot of it is thrown in the garbage, while here, children scrape pans off to collect a bean or a rice grain.

The Children's Calvary

Gisenyi, 18 November 1996

It is a sickening sight to see those sad faces of children who lost their parents and their acquaintances as well. These are moments one can never forget. Their looks are filled with all the grief of the tragedy they have been going through for over two years. Now, as they are finally coming back to their country, a new calvary is beginning for those who lost their beloved ones, and who actually do not know where to go or who to apply to. They are eagerly waiting for some of their relatives to come back and look for them. They do not realize that it is impossible to come back, as one would risk to be overwhelmed and crushed under foot by the crowd.

A loud-speaker keeps inviting children without parents to reach the collecting point. Within a few hours, there are hundreds of them, all frightened, crying, and calling their mom. Then, they sink in a corner, while eating greedily some cookies the volunteer nuns and missionaries, who operate in the area, have given them. These people are working to relieve the suffering of hundreds of thousands of refugees. Each child tells his or her own story about their flight from the Mugungwa camp, the rain, which relieved thirst on the one hand while making their way even more difficult on the other, intensified by tiredness and the pangs of hunger, which grew stronger and stronger. They have been walking for days with no rest at all to reach Rwanda. Many of them know the name of the village where they were born, they remember the green hills of Rwanda and their villages. Finding their parents again will be easier for them. But for those who cannot even say their own name, it will be a titanic undertaking to trace back their origins. My attention is being drawn to a child who is more or less seven years old. He is carrying a bag full of who-knows-what . I try to figure out its content. It is similar to other bags filled with poor things: a pan encrusted by many days of missing water, some wood chops, some filthy rags reduced to the mini- mum, a little tank without a cap, which will be of some use when collecting water along the way, some bottle caps, a piece of rope, a piece of an air tube, rags of what used to be a blanket, a piece of mat, a bucket, with its handle missing, some empty cans of tomato sauce, keys and plastic bags and a piece of sheeting. This is all the wealth that this nameless child, as he got lost in the mass, is carrying along with him. I will never forget his face or his eyes reddened by so much crying. While I approach him to ask him something, I realize that curious people are standing in a circle, other children are also standing round me and are looking at me. Some of them hide their eyes, someone else gives a glimpse of a smile, someone else stretches his or her hand out to me and all of them greets back. These children are hungry and their hearts are full of suffering. Their hands have not come in contact with any soap for several days. Some have wounds, which are slowly healing while risking to become infected if they do not undergo some care as soon as possible. Children like this one, who lost their parents, are more than 4 thousand within a few days of exodus. Fifty of these children will be welcomed in the Orphanage Mother of the Word in Kigali, which I founded and am managing. Here, they will find another 73 children who lived through their same tragedy two years ago, but who are now smiling because they have found a new large family. For sure, this will be an important event for the orphanage as well as a bigger task, which we hope to be able to carry out thanks to the generosity of our benefactors.

Mukamira, 19 November 1996

It's an all together different daybreak from the previous ones. A new day is starting for many people who have finally managed to sleep, after a long time, on the ground of their own homeland, while hoping to see their fields and their homes soon, if anything will have been left of them. People are coming and going. Within a few hours one cannot move because of the throng. New groups keep on arriving. We don't know how many of them have come so far. A lot of people have resumed their way to their original places before dawn.

The luckier ones are being driven by trucks, which the government, large organizations as well as private ones have made available. Each village is busy in preparing and organizing collecting camps to welcome new comers. Everyone will have to register at their original city hall where the city administration will have to solve all conflicts pertaining to properties. An enormous task, where it won't be easy to avoid low blows or personal revenges. For many of them, life will be difficult, for others it will be easier. On the whole national territory there will be work for all those people of good will who really wish to render a service. The GNO have an immense area to work on. It will be more difficult to tread on each other's toes in order to help other people. Areas requiring some intervention are so many that one will only have the embarrassment of knowing what to choose. It will also be interesting to see and appreciate the works they will be realizing. All this will help avoid any misunderstanding or any project for private convenience as well as unmask those organizations, which pretend to have humanitarian goals, but which are actually profiteering from others' troubles. They make unnecessary projects that are gigantic and fictitious and real only on paper so to obtain public funds. They are present on the tragedy spot only when everybody's attention is focused on that specific issue, while their only purpose is to fill their own pockets up before vanishing within a few moons carrying along all they could collect. Such organizations have appeared in Rwanda at the end of the 1994 war and within a few months they have disappeared, although someone has regularly come back to make their own scoops while stealing photographs and images somebody else had realized. The behavior of such questionable individuals is a far more serious tragedy than the refugees' one for humanity.

Mukamira, 20 November 1996

Those who happened to see a refugee camp may understand what it means. The pungent smell of human feces sticks to your throat and takes your breath away. People crowded together are being stricken by a frenetic activity to face the thousand and one needs, Children stick to their mothers' dress, boys are looking for anything that could be

158

of some use, old men sit apart to smoke their pipes, groups of men are bargaining, and women are either selling or bartering their few goods. But this time at the Mukamira camp, people are assaulting the vehicles, which should drive them to their own villages. Nobody expected so many people in such a hurry to reach their hills where they might find back something of what they once owned. It is the boarding of desperate people, who had been made ugly by distress. They fight to be the first one to climb onto these few means that will grant transportation to the next collecting points from where they will continue to their original villages. Because of such a throng, not everybody manages to step on to the emergency vehicle. Some family members are often left behind as they could not climb, while others have taken their place. Another tragedy begins. More families are being separated. I wonder whether and when they will ever join again. These kinds of tragedies are countless in Rwanda. There are thousands of them, considering the number of children who have been collected so far and who are hopelessly looking for their parents. Many of those who make it to here, because of their present conditions, will never again see their hills or their field. For them, the exodus finishes before they can reach their village, as they are worn out by tiredness and disease. One can count hundreds of corpses all along the street. They will be buried in one of the many common graves, which have been dug for the purpose. Poor people!

The Ghost of Hunger

Kigali, 21 November 1996

If news of the arrival of refugees has been accepted as a sign of peace for Rwanda on the one side, it has also caused the rise of prices of commodities one the other. A logical consequence, considering the request for these goods. If you browse around the Kigali markets, you can hear the comments while noticing the amazement of people who find out about the new prices. One goes back with half of the shopping necessary to feed their family; salaries have kept unchanged, and the only hope that has left is that the humanitarian help will arrive on time to satisfy the requirement of the market, cause the price decrease, and grant everybody his daily bread to the next harvest. We do hope that this time the decisions of the earth's big ones are taken in time and that help will come in time. All those who are coming back have to reach their village. It will take days before they can arrive and all along the street it is difficult to find shelter for so many people.

At the Mother of the Word orphanage, we have welcomed 56 children who lost their parents. They have come at seven o'clock, on three taxi-buses, having been accompanied by some agents of the Red Cross.

For our orphanage it is a hard task, but all of our children have shown maturity and concern, all of them, have done thier best to welcome the new comers, even the youngest ones, by greeting and welcoming them with a song.

Dinner was served with much delay to give everybody time to wash and use the bathrooms. Food was more than enough, only some forks or spoons were missing, but tomorrow we will solve this problem. In order to give everybody a bed, we had to move the refectory. The Kindergarten we inaugurated last 15 of August turned out to be a precious room and helped us solve many problems.

When looking at these children whose name is still unknown to me, but whose story I know, one may well understand how life has been difficult for them in these past years. They are dressed in a miserable way, wearing a filthy and creased shirt, a ragged pair of pants, they are barefoot and have been tossed around here and there. Among them, there is a 5 year old child who has been sorely tried by sufferings, and who has become so mature to leave us astonished. He is always playing with a piece of rope over which he rotates a piece of leaf. His story is the story of thousands of children who suffer because of war and hate. In these days, I am sure I will get to know many stories, which deserve to be told.

Kigali, at the Orphanage of the Mother of the Word, 22 November 1996

The night has gone by serenely. Children have found a hot meal and a mattress to sleep on with a

161

few blankets to sleep. They were exhausted. At last, a covered shelter. Our workers worked overtime. They all made themselves useful, they did all they could to make the environment as comfortable as it could be and the stay of these poor innocent children more serene.

In the morning, the children go to school, while the youngest ones stay home with the new comers. They drink some tea and have a sandwich. Finally, something different to eat: they do not leave a crumb, they have days in arrears with hunger to be filled. We leave for the market, We buy everything we can. We knock at some doors, but they hanged on their phones on us. We distribute new clothes, as the ones the children are wearing now are two years old and in rags: they can't even be washed. We have renovated most of them, our stock runs out quickly. Some of the children are sick, so we call a private doctor and pay for their visits. The medicines we don't have, we will buy at the pharmacy.

In the afternoon, we organize a soccer game. Everybody is part of one of the four teams. Eventually, the winners will gain three candies each, the other will have a few candies less. Everybody is happy. They hadn't had no moments of peacefulness for more than two years.

Father Vito Misuraca

Made and Printed in Italy
in april 1997
by INGRAF - Industria Grafica srl - Milan